MONTREAL AND THE FUR TRADE

E. E. RICH

MONTREAL AND THE FUR TRADE

Beatty Memorial Lectures

McGILL UNIVERSITY PRESS
MONTREAL
1966

381.439
R 37 m
57352
Mei. 1967

PRINTED IN GREAT BRITAIN
in 11 point Baskerville
BY LATIMER TREND & CO. LTD
PLYMOUTH

PREFACE

THE SIR Edward Beatty Memorial Lectures were established, through the generosity of Dr. Henry Beatty, as a memorial to his brother, the late Sir Edward Beatty, G.B.E., K.C., D.C.L., LL.D., formerly, and for more than twenty years, Chancellor of McGill University.

The Lectures are delivered by distinguished Visitors from outside of Canada and are open to the general public as well as to members and friends of the University.

The Lectures for the academic session of 1963–64 were delivered by Dr. Edwin Ernest Rich, Fellow and Master of St. Catharine's College, Cambridge, and Harmsworth Professor of Naval and Imperial History in the University of Cambridge. They offered a closely knit narrative of the role of Montreal in the North American fur trade from the days of Jacques Cartier to those of that James McGill who was the Founder of the University; and, in particular, they gave a fascinating account of the period between the American War of Independence and the 'coalition' between the North-west and the Hudson's Bay Companies; a period during which the Montreal men paid as scant attention, either to the frontier posts of the young republic or to the preserves of the Hudson's Bay Company, as their present-day descendants pay to the traffic regulations of their own city.

It was Dr. Beatty's wish, and it has always been our hope, that our Beatty Lecturers will not only deliver the statutory Lectures but will, also, remain with us, for as long as possible, and, during their stay, enter into the academic life of the University: and it is proper that I should record that Dr. Rich was exceptionally generous in the time which he gave both to members of staff and to the students of the University.

H. N. FIELDHOUSE
Vice-Principal (Academic)

CONTENTS

I

THE FRENCH BACKGROUND

A GREAT deal of painstaking and enterprising work has been done over the past fifty years on the history of the Canadian fur trade. It seems to me that much of it has two defects. Either it takes the fur trade as a series of economic abstractions—as a continuous succession of clashes between enterprise and monopoly, between capital concentrated and capital diffused, between price regulations and free marketing—or it gets so taken up with the vehement personalities involved in this trade that it rambles off into a series of ecstatic biographies. These are both aspects of Canadian fur-trade history which it would be folly to ignore. But the whole picture must be based upon underlying geographical facts.

Endless chapters have indeed been written upon the geographical background of the fur trade; and men who are really dour historians can get lyrical over the Great Shield of Canada, over the great river running away to the west, over the Laurentians, even over the muskegs. Such lyricism is apt to creep in when the geographical background is considered as background only, and not as the very basis of the trade. I shall try to emphasize in my three lectures the constant importance of this geographical factor; and I have devoted the first to the French régime because here the geographical factor, as it affected the French, is inescapably set out.

To the first French explorers of the sixteenth century, Canada was the land of the great river, the St. Lawrence; and conversely the St. Lawrence was the great river of Canada. It was 'the great River of Hochelaga [Montreal] and the route towards Canada'. To the north lay the Kingdom of Saguenay. Ultimately, the Frenchmen's attention was concentrated on breaking through the barrier of the Great Shield, which cut them off from that area and also from the west. Ultimately and of necessity, they concentrated on reaching out beyond the St. Lawrence valley towards the fur-bearing lands of the north and west. Initially, however, their interest lay in following the great river in the hope of finding a passage through America to the Pacific and to the spice lands beyond. That was the hope. The certainty was that the river would lead them to Hochelaga, to a considerable body of friendly Indians, and to a fertile and well-watered land.

So Jacques Cartier's second voyage brought him up the river to Hochelaga, where he found a great Huron village, probably on the site of this campus. He came early in October 1535, and, climbing the adjacent mountain which he named 'le Mont Royal', he gazed upon the fruitful land at his feet. His pinnaces lay at the foot of the 'courant Sainte-Marie'. This was 'ung sault d'eaue, le plus impétuaulx qu'il soit possible de veoir; lequel ne nous fut possible de passer'. The Hurons whom he met here told him that there were three such *saults,* after which the river would be easily navigable for a three months' journey to the west. The actual account which Jacques Cartier was given in 1535 is not very easy to reconcile with facts as we know them. But still, it left Cartier with a firm and, on the whole, justifiable notion of the land. To the north lay the Laurentians; to the south and the east, the Adirondacks and the Green Mountains. Between those two ranges lay great vistas of fertile land. Westward, at his feet, the great river flowed as far as the eye could see, 'grand, large et spaceiulx'.

Cartier in 1535, although he looked at the Sault and found it impassible, did not as yet accept it as the barrier to westward penetration by way of the St. Lawrence which it ultimately proved to be. In fact on his third voyage in 1541 he took two barques and tried to mount the sault. But although he then amalgamated his crews and put one boat on one side to reinforce the other, he found the first sault (which we know as Lachine Rapids) quite impossibly dangerous with its rocks and its strong currents. For his main purpose, which was to discover a route westward, that was enough. For this meant that at Montreal European ships, even European boats, had to be abandoned; further progress entailed portages, canoes, travelling in the Indian manner. The European had come to the head of navigation.

Cartier was amazed at the wealth of fur-bearing animals which he had seen in Canada, and at Montreal he had noted that the Hurons disposed of endless quantities of furs, although they lived by fishing and by agriculture. They never left their villages, they did not follow a wandering life, they didn't hunt the fur-bearing animals

themselves. On his second voyage he met a band of
Indians who had come to Montreal from the north,
from the Kingdom of Saguenay. They made him a present of three packs of furs and a great knife of copper
which they said came from the Kingdom of Saguenay.
So, Jacques Cartier was aware that here at the saults he
was not only at the head of European navigation, he
was also at the market end of a fur-trading route which
penetrated into the hinterland past the barriers which
held up the Europeans. He was aware that the St. Lawrence was unsuitable for further European travel. He
was aware that the route used by the Indians lay by way
of the Ottawa River, running westward under the
mountains to the north until it reached a great fresh-
water sea of which, as the Indians told him, no one had
ever seen the end. There, somewhere to the west or to
the northwest, lay the Kingdom of Saguenay, with its
furs and its copper, peopled by friendly Indians. But
Cartier was told that the Saguenay River itself, running
north from the lower St. Lawrence, soon became im-
passable except for canoes, that the journey from the
St. Lawrence to the Kingdom of Saguenay took a
month, and that the best route to this kingdom lay from
Montreal, not by the Saguenay, but by the Ottawa
River. It was reported to be a month's journey; and it
led to what ultimately proved to be Lake Huron.

On his third voyage, therefore, Cartier was not only
anxious to find out whether he could get his boats farther up the St. Lawrence, up the saults, and launched
once more on the great river to continue the journey
westward; he was also anxious to find out about other

rapids farther on, which he would have to overcome to get to the Kingdom of Saguenay; and he set to work for that purpose. But he was persuaded by the Hurons (who clearly did not want Cartier to venture any farther than the saults at Montreal) that the Ottawa River did not present a navigable route; and he gave up for the moment. In 1543 his successor, the Sieur de Roberval, took up Cartier's projects with more imposing strength and set forth for a voyage to the Kingdom of Saguenay with eight pinnaces. He also was held up at the Lachine Rapids. The crew which he sent on ahead obviously got wrecked on the rapids (because they were only at most two days absent from Montreal), and he lost one pinnace and eight men drowned. So Cartier and his immediate successor, Roberval, were halted at Montreal. Mount Royal marked the terminus of early French efforts to break out from Canada into Saguenay. It was already clear that the rapids marked not only the break-out point; they marked the terminus of an Indian trade route, the Ottawa River route followed by Indians coming down to trade with Europeans.

It was left to Samuel de Champlain, a half-century later, to break through the barrier which Cartier had met, to master the Ottawa River route. By Champlain's time the fur trade of Canada had already become a considerable industry whose growth had produced something of a new pattern of European trade. The main Canadian arteries of that trade ran down from the Kingdom of Saguenay to Tadoussac by the Saguenay River, and trade to Europeans lay largely in the hands of the Montagnais and the Algonquin tribes who used that route. They annually brought the furs of the north and west to barter at Tadoussac; and much as Samuel de Champlain wrote, much as he undoubtedly felt, about exploration, colonization, civilization of North America and Canada, there is very little doubt that his plans and proposals centred around the fur trade. In fact his first voyage to Canada in 1603 was organized because of protests by French merchants about the mishandling of that trade. Champlain, in order to get away from rivals in the lower St. Lawrence and Tadoussac, broke away, brought a twelve-ton pinnace up the river as far once more as the Lachine Rapids—as far as Cartier had got. Here, he also was halted. Here, he also was fed upon Indian rumours of rivers, rapids, and ultimately of a great sea, the far shore of which had never been seen. By this time the Hurons whom Cartier had met in Hochelaga had been driven away. They had deserted this site, driven westward by the remorseless opposition of the Iroquois, the Five Nations. Even Cartier perhaps did not meet them on his second voyage, though he certainly met them on his first. But the Indian reports and eye-witnesses' accounts which Champlain got were very much the same as those which Cartier had met. Champlain also landed, he also inspected the rapids, and he also found them so dangerous that it was beyond the power of man to pass with any boat.

For Champlain also, Lachine Rapids, the saults, were the end of European navigation. But Champlain, who incidentally could not swim, was in the end to run the Lachine Rapids downstream in an Indian canoe in 1611, the first white man to do so and survive. He was also, in 1613, to show his growing confidence in canoe travel, venturing by portage up past the rapids to Lac St. Louis, to Lac des Deux Montagnes, to Rideau Falls in the present city of Ottawa, to Lac des Chats, then to the stronghold of the Algonquin Indians on Lac des Alumettes. Champlain was ultimately to have enough competence in canoe travel to push his way past the barrier of the rapids and to make Frenchmen masters of the Ottawa River route to the west. Where Jacques Cartier had been halted at Montreal, Champlain, using canoes, ultimately mastered the rapids and opened the Ottawa River route.

Two years later, in 1615, Champlain opened still wider vistas when he followed the headlong Recollect missionaries along the same route to Lac des Alumettes, farther west by the Mattawa River to Lake Nipissing, and so by French River (breaking through the Shield) down to Georgian Bay and Lake Huron. Champlain, in this voyage by the Ottawa River to Lake Huron, had caught up with the Huron tribes. He had opened the way for Frenchmen to follow the routes which led from Huronia, through the Straits of Mackinac to Lake Michigan, to Green Bay, to the woods and plains of Wisconsin, to Illinois, and to the sources of the Missouri. He had also opened the way past Sault Ste. Marie to Lake Superior, so to Kaministikwia, the Grand Rapid, Rainy Lake, Cedar Lake, the Saskatchewan and the northwest. They all followed (not in his time it is true) from his opening of the Ottawa route. From Lake Huron a route would lead eastward again, by the Detroit (the narrows into Lake Erie) to Niagara and

Lake Ontario, and by the St. Lawrence back to Montreal once more.

Champlain and his patrons had turned the head of navigation at Lachine into an intermediate stage for French expansion. They had also turned it into a great annual rendezvous for the fur trade. As they were opening the way westward they were making confident arrangements, sometimes overconfident, for Indians to bring their furs down year by year. The great annual fur-trade rendezvous in Montreal was in part an effort to escape from competitors on the lower St. Lawrence at Tadoussac, competitors who met the Indians and traded for their furs. When Champlain's rivals in trade followed him to his rendezvous with the Indians at Mount Royal, he had gone up the Ottawa, then on into Huronia, pushing the frontiers of the fur trade ahead of him. He did this partly because the independent traders worried the Indians, and drove them away from the rendezvous, partly because he wanted to explore and find the northern sea which was reputed to be within reasonable distance of the rapids, partly because he wished to break through a most unmistakable cordon of Indian middlemen and to get to the sources of the furs which were brought down to the St. Lawrence.

Cartier in his time had been well aware that the Montagnais and Algonquins who brought furs down to trade were for the most part middlemen, and that they were not anxious that he should break through and reach the Kingdom of Saguenay. Indeed they opposed him. Champlain had exactly the same conviction, and he established the reason for that conviction in greater detail. From the lower St. Lawrence, Champlain was anxious to get up to the Kingdom of Saguenay, but he found the Saguenay River difficult, as Cartier had been warned that it was. Also he found, as Cartier had found, that he was being constantly fobbed off by Indians who wished him *not* to try to explore northward from the lower St. Lawrence. Similarly, when he got to Lac des Alumettes and met the Algonquins in their stronghold there, he found that tribe commanding the route down to the trade fair on the St. Lawrence at Montreal and living well despite the poverty of their soil. He found too, that they were full of objections against any proposal that he should push on and visit the Nipissings, who lived six days journey to the west. When eventually, in 1615, he broke through the Algonquins and actually met the Nipissings, he found that they were not fur hunters either. They too, the Nipissings, were a great nation of traders, whose buyers (there is no other word for it) habitually travelled westward to Sault Ste. Marie, to Lake Superior, and even northward towards Hudson's Bay, exchanging European trade goods, which had come up by the Ottawa route from Montreal, for the furs which they then passed to the Hurons and the Algonquins, who brought them down to Montreal.

So what had been strongly suspected by Cartier, and what was revealed in detail by Champlain, was that the European rendezvous at Montreal lay at the far end of a highly complicated and closely controlled Indian trade system. Despite their apparently different sense of values and their different notions of buying and selling, of giving goods in gift exchange, and so on, the Indians

B

with whom the Europeans were making contact were professional traders.

The tribal alliances and hostilities to which the French were committed during Champlain's régime were to last throughout their rule in Canada and were to affect all that the French did. They were in particular to make it possible and desirable for Frenchmen to live with Indians, to travel with them and adopt their ways, to use (and on the whole to use profitably) the knowledge of this country which the Indians possessed. That knowledge was extensive and accurate. But theories began where knowledge stopped—at the eastern end of Lake Superior—and the French adopted the theories also. These theories proved misleading and dangerous; but if we distinguish theory from statement of fact and confine ourselves to what the Indians said as being within their knowledge, we must be impressed with the information which Champlain and his men got by this means.

They also got the habit of living and travelling with Indians; and the *coureur de bois*, who epitomized this aspect of French life, and of the French fur trade in particular, was inaugurated by Champlain himself. For Champlain sent a very boastful and deceitful young man, one De Vignau, on a journey to the northern sea, a journey which De Vignau never undertook although he pretended he did. Champlain also sent Etienne Brulé to spend the winter of 1610–11 up the Ottawa with the Algonquins. Brulé was then only seventeen years old, a young man who became so accustomed to Indian ways of life that he went native with a vengeance. He was ultimately executed by his Indian blood brothers—for what crimes we are not told. Champlain sent a young man, probably Brulé once more, to winter at Lake Huron and find out the route before he went there himself. He then sent him south from Lake Erie, through Iroquois territory, to the Andastes. It was Brulé who travelled along the north shore of Lake Huron to Sault Ste. Marie and came back to the white settlements with the first positive news of Lake Superior seen by a white man's eyes. Young men such as Brulé travelled with the Indians, lived with them, accepted them, and were accepted by them; they were the first coureurs de bois.

In all this, Champlain was accepting the head of navigation at the rapids as a focal point from which the French must spread outward; a focal point, also, to which the Indians would converge. He was therefore constantly developing means of enticing the Indians down to trade and of allowing the French to spread outward. At Montreal he planned a permanent settlement. In 1611 he selected the site and even began a building which he called Place Royal, just back from the river on the site of the present Customs House. But no city was built in his time. Not until 1642 did the dedicated missionary movement which originated in the church of St. Sulpice in Paris found a city on this site. But when Ville Marie was established, in that year, it immediately emphasized the inescapable importance of the position which Champlain had chosen. The site was probably taken from Champlain's own recommendation, and the first buildings used, as their fortification, wooden stakes which he had cut. For this site was at once the strategic centre of defence against the Iroquois, the point of departure for all western and northern journeys, and the rendezvous to which the trading Indians brought their annual flotillas of furs. Quebec, Tadoussac, and Trois-Rivières, lower down the St. Lawrence, retained much importance. But Montreal quickly won pride of place; quickly but not immediately, for Montreal was in the forefront against the Iroquois and its trade was easily interrupted. In alliance with the Dutch, and later with the English, the Iroquois were anxious to break the French fur trade and to lead the furs down the Hudson River to the English and the Dutch settlements. They were bitterly and inescapably committed to warfare against the Hurons, the Algonquins, and all the tribes within the French alliance; and they had been embroiled in hostilities against the French by Champlain himself, for he had taken part in the wars against the Iroquois.

The Iroquois power lay over the whole land, from Lake Huron to Tadoussac. The trade of the Montagnais down from Saguenay was already worked out. By 1650 there were no Indians living along the route of the Ottawa River. The surviving Hurons had either been driven from Lake Huron farther westward into Wisconsin or they had fled for protection to the French in such fear that they would not even stop at Montreal but continued downriver all the way to Quebec, there to live on charity. Here, at Montreal, 'one saw nothing but enemies every day, no one dared to open his door by night, and in the day time no one dared to go more than four steps from his house without being armed with musket, sword and pistol'. The Iroquois formally attacked the settlement in 1642, the year of foundation; they attacked again in 1643, and in almost every subsequent year. It was in fact a militant theocracy which maintained Montreal.

But inauspicious though the times might be for the foundation of a permanent settlement at Montreal, the enterprise not only continued but flourished. It was above all things a bastion of Christianity. But its survival was also due to the lure of the fur trade, and to the position of Montreal in that fur trade. The Compagnie de la Nouvelle France, which Richelieu had founded in 1627 with the purpose of using the fur trade to underwrite the establishment of a populous colony, fell upon evil times. It lost money in many years. Yet by 1645, whatever the company might be suffering, the profits from the trade were such that a group of the habitans contracted to take over control of the trade with the right to make their own regulations; and the small group which was thus formed in its turn made such profit in its first year (about 320,000 livres) that the generality of the habitans, not merely a small clique, clamoured for a share. So in 1647 a general freedom of trade was secured for all the French habitans of the country to trade in skins and furs with the Indians. Thus, as Montreal was struggling into existence, the habitan was struggling for existence as an individual fur trader, out of the control of any company and prepared to undertake payment of the necessary costs of the colony in return for participation in that trade. This meant that the trade was closely enmeshed with government and that government depended closely upon the fur trade. It proved in fact difficult if not impossible to balance dues and costs of administration against profits, just as difficult to balance profits from the trade against the purchases from France of annual supplies of food which were still necessary. Adjustments were made in 1648, in 1652, and again in 1653. By that time government intervention had brought the value of the trade down from 250,000 livres a year to about 65,000, and in 1660, the habitans sold out their position to a Compagnie de Normandie, a company of speculators, which agreed to pay the debts which the habitans had incurred and to underwrite the costs of administration. In 1663, the Compagnie de la Nouvelle France, from whose original grant the whole thing had stemmed, was itself taken over and abolished.

During this period the complicated manœuvres of the different companies matter very little. What does matter is that the habitan, the ordinary colonist as an individual, was vindicating his freedom to participate in the fur trade against the monopoly of a privileged company; and that the fur trade and its profits were the mainstay of the life of the colony, upon which the costs of administration were based. It is exceedingly difficult to gauge the place of Montreal in this development. Certainly, Quebec was predominant over Montreal as late as 1647, at the time the habitans first took over the trade. But Montreal was only five years old at that time, and it was a very troublesome five years which it had just survived. Still, the Governor of Montreal's salary, and pay for a garrison of thirty soldiers, were accepted as standing charges against the colony's revenue. The details were revised in the following year, 1648, when all expenses were scaled down and the garrison at this outpost was reduced to a mere six soldiers. But whether its garrison was set at six soldiers or thirty, Montreal was written into the development of the colony. The representative system which was developing for the government of the colony acknowledged not only the comparative importance of Montreal as a centre of settlement, but also the rising importance of the individual habitan, the coureur de bois who set out from Montreal. And having survived its first trials, Montreal in fact showed considerable and rapid increase. The seigneuries along the riverfront were granted away under Governor Jean de Lauzon (from 1651 to 1656). During that period a reinforcement of about a hundred men was brought out from France in 1653—as contemporaries said, 'none save men of spirit and ability to carry out their orders'—and these hundred men marked the turning-point in the early history of the town; for the attacks of the Iroquois were held from 1653 onwards. In the next year, in 1654, a shipload of 'honest girls' was brought out to comfort the men of spirit, and in 1659 a further recruitment of a hundred men and women came; the colony was on its feet.

During the period 1642 to about 1660, as the Compagnie des Habitans came and went, the coureurs de bois steadily went on trading furs. Whatever the law said, the soldiers, the honest girls, the men of spirit arrived, and the Iroquois menace was held. During this period the narratives are very much taken up with personal adventures, and the formal documents with regulations and with agreements, legal and territorial. It is difficult, at times impossible, to ascertain facts which we should expect to be obvious and which I think are important—facts such as the date at which the annual trade fair developed into a permanently open *magasin*. The trade fair as established by Champlain was a rendezvous at which French traders who never left Montreal met Indians who brought down furs. These were for the most part Indian middlemen who came down to the Lachine Rapids with furs which they in turn had traded. That rendezvous at some time developed into a permanent magasin at which French traders who had gone into the woods brought down, and paid in, the furs which they had themselves brought from the pays d'en haut. That is an important change; but goodness knows when it took place. It had certainly happened by 1652, because in that year the Iroquois were roaming again and the *Jesuit Relations* describes the happiness of the beavers, left in their dams undisturbed by the hunters, enjoying their repose; and not a solitary skin was brought down to the magasin at Montreal. So, by 1652, although no beaver was brought into it, there was a warehouse or permanent store, replacing the trade fair, on which the trade converged.

The permanent magasin was accompanied by an increase in the importance of the French fur trader. The arrival of reinforcements at Montreal in 1653 and 1654 not only allowed the Iroquois menace to be halted, it also allowed the individual habitan to use Montreal as a base from which trade could be driven past the Iroquois cordons into the pays d'en haut, into the Indian country which began at the rapids. In that year the Iroquois made some sort of peace with the French, and Governor de Lauzon took the opportunity to send two young Frenchmen westward in company with the Hurons and Ottawas. Those tribes had sent down to the St. Lawrence in 1653 to report that the nations scattered by the Iroquois were awaiting French traders, and they had brought some furs down in 1654. The Indians with whom the two young Frenchmen went westward in 1654 were Ottawa Indians, the *cheveux relevés* whom Champlain had met at Mackinac and at Manitoulin Island as he came down the French River in 1613. These Ottawa Indians controlled the Ottawa River by the 1660's, for the Hurons and Algonquins had been driven west; and since the Ottawas controlled the river they controlled the approach to Montreal, and so they controlled French trade. Like so many Indians with whom the Europeans came in contact, the Ottawas were trading Indians. In 1654 they were at the beginning of their careers as merchants, to some extent replacing the Hurons and standing out against the Iroquois for access to Montreal and the French market. They needed French help, and they were able to bring life-giving supplies of furs to Montreal. By 1662, the Ottawas had extended their trade system to the north, and northern tribes, especially the Crees of the far north, can be seen engaged in systematic hunting to provide furs to trade with the Ottawas, who would bring them down to the Montreal market. The stimulant of the whole process was French goods, which the

Ottawas got in Montreal. Within another generation, by 1681, the Ottawas had almost a monopoly; other tribes seldom or never made the long journey down to the settlements. So, as the Jesuits reported, 'Although they for the most part do not hunt, and have but a small portion of peltry in their country,' the Ottawas got their peltry 'in the north from the people of the interior' and exchanged it 'for our merchandise, which they procure at Montreal'.

It was, then, with the Ottawas that two young Frenchmen went westward in 1654. They went from Montreal, the place where the Ottawas brought their furs and bought their goods. For just as Montreal had been the centre of French resistance during the period of the Iroquois threat, so it was the centre for French advance during the period after 1654 when the French stabilized their position and began once more to advance. That advance consisted in something more than merely an alliance with the Ottawas, more than exploitation of the trading genius of the Ottawas, to stimulate the flow of furs to Montreal. These two young Frenchmen who went westward in 1654, seeking the pays d'en haut, were in a great tradition. They were perhaps sent expressly by the Governor, Jean de Lauzon. They certainly went with his blessing and his knowledge. One of them was Jean Baptiste Groseillers. He comes into the history of the Hudson's Bay Company as Mr. Gooseberry; and as Mr. Gooseberry he plays a vital part in the history of that company. Who went with him in 1654 is uncertain. But it was not Pierre Esprit Radisson (although Radisson later pretended that it was he), for Radisson was somewhere else at the time. Apart from Radisson it could have been any one of a score of men, because the chronicle says 'all our young Frenchmen are planning to go on a trading expedition, to find the Nations that are scattered here and there.' These young men, of whom we can put our fingers on two in 1654, were the descendants of Champlain's young men, of the coureurs de bois whom he had started, ready to travel with Indians and to bring them down to trade. There would be no lack of companions for Groseillers.

There can be no doubting the part played by Montreal in this development. Shortly after this particular episode of 1654, during his first governorship, Frontenac wrote that more Indians were coming down to Montreal than ever before, as many as eight hundred Ottawas at a time. The coureurs de bois had started the flow of trade, carrying French goods into the upper territories while the Ottawas and others were bringing down their furs. All were converging on Montreal. Here, the great rendezvous, the trade fairs which Champlain had initiated, for a short time assumed an ever-increasing importance as the Ottawa flotillas came in growing numbers. But before the close of the century the coureurs had established regular routes to Lake Superior, and from Kaministikwia, northwards to Rainy Lake, to which they had penetrated by 1688. Although they found that the intermediate trading tribes with whom they travelled were anxious as ever to prevent French access to the more distant fur-hunting tribes, and though they became involved in endless tribal quarrels as well as in the long-term hostilities with the Iroquois, yet they kept thrusting outwards. Always they had Montreal as their starting point, with the Ottawa River as their initial step upon the journey.

As the coureurs' trade spread, entrepôts developed at focal points like Detroit, Sault Ste. Marie, or Mackinac. But although those entrepôts undoubtedly made it easier for French coureurs to outfit themselves up-country, giving them more time for their trade or for their voyages, and though they intercepted Indians coming down to Montreal's trade fairs (which for this reason began to decline), yet they served merely as outposts for Montreal and enhanced its importance. For Montreal was the transhipment point at which bulk was broken and the cargoes for the upper country were made up to be transported by canoes. Montreal still offered the basic advantages which it had always offered. It was a control point at the foot of the Ottawa River. That river offered a route which was now practicable for Europeans, and which also took the traders northward out of the territory dominated by the Iroquois. For that reason Montreal and the Ottawa River fitted into the pattern of Indian warfare and rivalry.

In all of this Montreal had its own difficulties. The cost of European goods was high, and, above everything, there were far too many coureurs out in the woods. The furs coming down were, in fact, causing a glut on the markets of Europe. The coureurs' trade was therefore challenged both because the coureur so easily evaded controls, monopolies, and taxation, and also because his trade was held to debauch both Frenchmen and Indians. He debauched Frenchmen by accustoming them to live with Indians in the fullest sense of the word (particularly, of course, with Indian women), and Indians by trading on their insatiable thirst for alcohol. The two problems caused a great rift in the colony; but in the end a General Assembly, convened at Quebec in 1678, confirmed the habitans in what was called their *commerce de boissons*, and the coureurs continued. But the dangers of this trade, and indeed of the coureurs as a whole, were nevertheless to be mitigated by making the trade public, by forbidding the habitan to take spirits inland to trade with the Indians 'in their habitations'; for it was held that the Indians would be in less danger if the trade had to be conducted in public. This was a compromise which was acceptable to the clergy, if it could be enforced. But if the veto upon taking spirits to trade in the Indian habitations meant that the coureurs were expected to trade without taking spirits inland, this would have amounted to a veto upon the coureurs' trade, since Indians would not trade without a dram. As a veto on taking spirits inland, therefore, the compromise was laughed out of court. The discussion nevertheless throws a valuable light on the fur trade because knowledgeable traders insisted that there was a great difference between trading spirits for furs and giving the Indian a drink and then trading his furs. The distinction may seem meaningless, but in view of the Indians' notions of value, of trade, of buying and selling and gift exchange, the distinction between trading spirits and making a gift of a dram has more weight than we are inclined to ascribe to it. But it left the fur trade dependent on spirits, and increasingly in the hands of coureurs who journeyed upcountry in search of furs. Naturally, and almost inevitably, the situation developed by 1681 (for example) to a point at which the Intendant reported that although only twenty-five licences were officially granted to coureurs in any one year, yet at a minimum estimate there were always about five hundred Frenchmen in the woods. In 1693 the Intendant reported that he had only licensed the departure of twenty-five canoes; but a hundred and eighty-seven had just come in, all laden with furs. So restrictions on the coureurs, for a variety of reasons, never worked. They remained nevertheless a constant feature of the French colony and were a source of continual friction. The Intendants maintained that the Governors connived at the coureurs, and the Governors protested that the Intendants supported them, each hinting that the other was well paid for so doing.

The habitans continued to abandon their houses and the cultivation of their lands; and a pattern of the French fur trade developed in which the coureurs de bois became essential to the very existence of the colony, and ability to direct and control them became a major problem of policy. Having failed to suppress or to control the coureurs, the French, in a realistic manner, tried to use and direct them. In particular, they tried to direct them towards Hudson's Bay and the northwest. This policy was undertaken by Frontenac and supported (in his own way) by his successor, De la Barre; and it brought great trouble to the Hudson's Bay Company who reckoned that it took about £20,000 worth of fur a year from their markets. It is astonishing, considering the distances involved, that the Hudson's Bay trade and any trade that in those days could be reached by way of the Ottawa should have affected each other. But the sea route to Hudson's Bay gave the English company an enormous advantage in that sea-going ships made it possible for them to bring in heavy goods. It is easy to make too much of that factor, because the English trade grew in the shadow of the French coureurs (it was largely instigated by Mr. Gooseberry and Pierre Esprit Radisson, two French coureurs de bois) and it aimed to offer the Indians an alternative supply of the goods which they had learned to desire rather than to develop different and new requirements. Consequently much of the English ships' cargoes, when we examine the bills of lading, was made up of light goods, spirits, tobacco, beads, such as the coureurs could carry inland, and which they had taught the Indians to want. But there were also bolts of woollen cloth, blankets, ironware, traps, hatchets, guns and shot, which the coureur could not take to the upper country in any quantity in his birchbark canoe. Those heavy goods the English supplied at the Bay, and with those heavy goods they encouraged the Indians to come and to trade. They were reluctant to travel inland themselves and the English pattern of trade was quite different from that which the French coureurs from Montreal had worked out. The English pattern was to entice the Indians down to trade at the Bay, the French pattern was to go and seek the Indian in his habitation and to trade with him there. The English pattern depended upon reaching

past the cordon of trading Indians and getting to the
real fur hunters. But the fur hunters on whom both
patterns were dependent were the same; in large part
they were the Crees, the Cristinos, of the barren north
lands. So, different though the patterns of trade were, it
was inevitable that the trade posts of the English on
Hudson's Bay must affect Montreal. For, like the
French trade, the English trade was integrated into a
continental scheme of Indian life. The final arrival of a
flotilla of canoes at Port Nelson or Fort James was, like
the final arrival of a flotilla at Montreal, the last stage of
a complex system which reached perhaps as far inland
as the Rockies, and which certainly reached to Lake
Winnipeg, to Cedar Lake, and the Saskatchewan.

News travelled fast in such a system, and competition
ramified with amazing speed and complexity. The
pioneer voyage of the English company to Hudson's Bay
in 1670 was a small venture by any standards, two small
ships and an indifferent assortment of goods. But the
Algonquins brought the news to Tadoussac, and by
November of that year the French Intendant, Talon,
had developed a plan to counter the move and had sent
it off to France. The English trade nevertheless persisted
and its influence spread; for example, in 1673, only
three years later, Frontenac received a report from a
mission priest at Sault Ste. Marie, which made it clear
that the English influence had upset trade in and
around Lake Superior. The report, from a great distance
from the Bay, proved that English influence had penetrated right across the central region of Lake Winnipeg.

The early lists of the tribes who came to the Bay were

of course lists drawn up by Englishmen who were un-accustomed to Indians and whose designation of the tribes cannot be completely relied upon. Nevertheless they not only included Eskimos and Nodways (from the Nodway River near the Bay) and Crees (the Cristinos who hunted the lands north of Winnipeg), they also included (and the English cannot have made the names up) the Assinipoets or the Stone Indians of the Saskatchewan, the Algonquins, the Micmacks, and the Ottawas themselves. There can be very little reason to doubt that tribes from well within the French fur-catchment area were not only affected by the Bayside trade but even the great Ottawa middlemen themselves went down to the Bay. All were definitely affected by the English posts on the Bay.

As with most problems of life in Canada under the ancien régime, this problem of resisting the remote effects of the English on Hudson's Bay became enmeshed in personalities, in politics, and probably in corruption. It produced a great deal of recrimination. It bedevilled the whole life of Canada, the church, the administrative system, agriculture and settlement, the solvency of the colony, the manners, the morals, the way of life of the whole people. It became involved in the warfare be-tween the two great European countries; and it produced a quite inexplicable economic outcome. For the fur trade upon which it all turned was a finely balanced technical process; so much so that government attempts to set rules and to adjust prices were doomed to failure. In the last resort the trade had to be geared to the markets of Europe. European hatters required one-quarter of parchment beaver (that is the ordinary sun-cured beaver skin) and three-quarters of coat. Coat beaver was, as its name implies, a beaver skin which the Indian had worn as a coat. He had worn it through the winter and had imparted a certain amount of animal fat to it. The coat had become greasy and supple by wear; it had lost some of its coarser guard hairs and consisted almost entirely of the soft underfur, called *duvet* by the French, which was greatly valued by felters. But parchment beaver was the great commodity of the St. Lawrence trade which the habitan conducted and which the coureurs brought in. The Indians who supplied the St. Lawrence trade did not know how to *engraisser* (how to grease up) their skins, though the process was simple enough; and so the St. Lawrence trade brought in infinitely more parchment than coat. Yet the Paris hatter wanted three times as much coat as parchment. The French trade was out of phase. Nevertheless the habitan had to be kept going, and the trade had to be run so that Canada could pay its way. Contractors were indeed found who would undertake to run the fur trade, to make a profit out of it, and to pay the revenues of Canada. But one after another the contractors went bankrupt.

It was in fact a sick and disjointed fur trade upon which the economy of Canada rested and which the active community of Montreal was expanding so dangerously. By 1696 it was estimated that the annual product of this trade was up to 150,000 pounds. But the annual demand of the French hatters was only 60,000 pounds. The fur trade was overproducing. Worse, it was producing the wrong qualities of fur in the wrong quantities; and it was the only trade which Canada had. By 1699 it seemed that the only possible remedy was a complete veto on all the coureurs. This would mean a veto on the whole trade, and the prospect could not be faced. Instead, the habitans were given complete freedom to trade. This also was a desperate remedy, and the result was that a vast mass of unsaleable skins poured into the magasin, rotten, moth-eaten, maggoty. The *amas furieux*, the insensate, crazy collection of furs, piled up, stinking, in the warehouses. All possible markets were fully stocked for years ahead; and by 1703, by which time warfare had begun to interrupt the trade still further, Vaudreuil could only advocate that all coureurs should be pulled in from their trade and supplies of furs should be ruthlessly cut. The economy was glutted with beaver. Year after year the colony was producing more than France could either use or export. Whether the remedy lay in a free market, in adjustment in the control of prices, in pronouncing sentence of death upon the coureurs, or in offering them a free pardon (and both were freely discussed) were open questions hotly disputed.

This economic situation is still largely inexplicable; but it was essential for the French to attempt an explanation and a remedy, because from the start of the eighteenth century policy took hold, and the fur trade became a factor in the intercolonial rivalry between French and English. The fur-trade routes became the boundaries of colonial expansion, taking the French to strategic positions on the back and at the flank of the

English colonies. The route from Lake Ontario to Lake Champlain and from there to Ticonderoga (the Mohawk Trail) became the invasion route by which the French, travelling swiftly and silently with their Indian allies, raided the English colonies. The Great Lakes and the Mississippi became the route by which the successors of La Salle moved in the opposite direction from that pioneer, no longer from Canada down into Louisiana but from Florida up into Arkansas and Michigan and, once more, to the back of the English colonies. By 1732 the English Board of Trade noted that the French, by huts and fur posts and forts, had managed 'to establish a communication between their Territories on the Continent of America, which lye on the Back of the English Settlements from the entrance of the River St. Lawrence to the mouth of the Mississippi.' The coureurs played their part although they often took their furs to the English market and got supplies from the English, and although during the wars Montreal was cut off from European goods so that it could not be an effective organizing centre for this trade. Control of the trade and of the Indians who depended on it lay so much in French hands that, by the time the clash of the great colonial powers came, the French Governor, in 1745, was not only able to give the hatchet to his own Indians (to join them, as he said, in a 'mutual defence' against the English), he was even able to offer the hatchet to the English allies, the Iroquois.

Much of the trade came from the Great Lakes, Lake Michigan, the head waters of the Missouri or the Mississippi, and the lands at the back of the English colonies;

and French fur traders went from Montreal in that direction. More important, particularly for one interested in the Hudson's Bay Company, was the development of what came to be called the *postes du nord*. North from Lake Superior, by Kaministikwia, by the portages over the Height of Land to Rainy Lake, and to Lake Winnipeg, lay the routes by which the Crees reached the Nelson and Churchill Rivers running down to Hudson's Bay and the English posts. As the French moved round by sea or overland from Quebec to absorb those English posts, they also set out to control this route from Kaministikwia. As policy took hold of the French fur trade, in 1716, the Governor and the Intendant composed a memorial advocating French expansion northwest from Kaministikwia through Lake of the Woods to Lake Winnipeg. From there, they said, a river flowed to the Sea of the West. Now the Sea of the West by 1716 was beginning to become a myth even for the French. But English rivalry was not. And the fur trade was not; it was in a mess but it was not a myth. So the Governor, Vaudreuil, proposed that, to control this all-important fur-trade route, three posts, the postes du nord, should be built. One post, the spring board, was to be at Kaministikwia, where Pigeon River runs into Lake Superior; the next post was to be at Rainy Lake, half-way to Lake Winnipeg, and the third (the geography was a little vague) somewhere on Lake Winnipeg. That was Vaudreuil's theory; and that was the purpose taken up in 1727 when Pierre Gaultier de Varennes, Sieur de la Vérendrye, became commandant of the postes du nord. Something had in the meantime been accomplished towards the fulfilment of Vaudreuil's plan. In 1717 the small post at Kaministikwia had been developed into a defensible fort by de la Nouë, an outpost at Rainy Lake was set up in 1718, and under de la Nouë's successor (Deschaillons) a post at Nipigon was also brought under control. A distant Hudson's Bay trader reported that 'the Strange Indians informed me that several of the French Canadians . . . have several places well fortified . . . and are well stored with all trading goods for the natives and have drawn most part of those Indians to them that used to come here to trade.' But before Vérendrye's time the trade to these posts was negligible —three canoes to Kaministikwia in 1723, a canoe and five men to Nipigon in that year, a solitary canoe to Kaministikwia in 1724 and again in 1725, and only three canoes in 1728. The Sioux were at war with the Crees and the Assiniboines, and de la Nouë was a disappointed man when he handed over his command.

The story of Vérendrye and his sons is one which has been fully worked over. As Commandant of the postes du nord he secured the approval of Governor Beauharnois and then, in 1731, made an agreement with a powerful group of Montreal merchants for the establishment of a post at Lake of the Woods. In that year he himself got no farther than Grand Portage on Lake Superior. But his nephew set up a fort at Rainy Lake, and in 1732 Vérendrye established Fort Charles at Lake of the Woods. He sent on scouts to Lake Winnipeg in 1733, and in 1734, while Vérendrye went to Montreal to quiet his creditors, his son Pierre and his partner René

Cartier set up Fort Maurepas on Lake Winnipeg.

So far, Vérendrye had driven his posts to the outfall of Red River, of the Assiniboine, and even of the Saskatchewan, and had brought the trade of those rivers into the orbit of Montreal in a new and organized way. His posts were an answer to the problems posed by the fact that it was impossible to get from Montreal to Lake Winnipeg in one summer. They made it possible for the coureurs to be outfitted in the pays d'en haut, and so to penetrate farther afield.

But such a system called for powerful financial support; and by 1734 Vérendrye had brought but little profit to his partners, and he had not discovered a route to the Sea of the West. He was forced to hand over control of his trade for a three years' period, and when he returned to the postes du nord in 1736 he was held up by the death of his nephew and by the massacre of a party under the command of his eldest son, at Lake of the Woods. It was 1738 before he could set off to seek the Sea of the West by visiting the much-rumoured Mandan villages and the 'Rivière des Mandans, qu'on croît être le Missouri'. His journey led from Lake Winnipeg by way of the Assiniboine, and when he returned in 1739 he was not only broken in health and disappointed that many of the Mandan rumours had proved false; he was also convinced that exploration southwest from Lake Winnipeg would be unprofitable.

So the western feeders of Lake Winnipeg were explored—first the Rivière Blanche, which is the outfall of the Saskatchewan, and then Lake Manitoba. His posts multiplied—Fort la Reine at Portage la Prairie, Fort

Bourbon at Cedar Lake—but he was beset by financial troubles and by Indian wars, and it was 1742 before he could organize another great voyage to confirm his ideas. Then two of his sons, Louis-Joseph and François, set off from Fort la Reine (Portage la Prairie) and travelled first south to the Mandans again, then west across the Bad Lands of the Little Missouri, and so, probably, to the foot of the Rockies. Their journey is difficult to establish in detail, but on their return they certainly travelled through South Dakota, for they buried a leaden plaque at St. Pierre, South Dakota, on 30 March 1743—and it has recently been dug up there.

The romance of this journey is only too apt to obscure its serious importance. For it emphasized the conclusion that further exploration to the south of west would be fruitless. The true direction lay north of west, up the Saskatchewan. Vérendrye himself did not live to see the fulfilment of his plans, for he was superseded in 1744; and, although he was again appointed to the postes du nord in 1749, he was then too ill to reach his command; he died at Montreal in December 1749. His sons were passed over in favour of forceful but inexperienced officers. But even under such management the French mastered the Saskatchewan. Fort Paskoyac was built at the mouth of Carrot River in 1750, and from there a party went on a further seven hundred miles or so—perhaps by the South Branch to the foot of the Rockies, perhaps by the North Branch to somewhere near Calgary. Fort La Corne (whose site is hotly disputed) was established upstream of Paskoyac to confirm that the postes du nord had given the drainage areas of Lake Winnipeg and of the Saskatchewan into the control of the French traders from Montreal.

Here, with Vérendrye and his successors, is the third geographical development of the French régime. The first, with Cartier, brought the French to the head of navigation at Lachine, and stopped them there. The second, with Champlain, opened the way westward and southward, past the barrier of the saults and past the barriers both of the Iroquois and of the trading Indians. The third, on the eve of the British conquest of Canada, took Frenchmen over the Grand Portage and the Height of Land to the Saskatchewan. This brought the French trade, and the merchants of Montreal, into constant rivalry with Hudson's Bay.

Suggestions for further reading:

BEAUCHESNE, Th., Ch.–A. JULIEN, and R. HERVAL. 'Les Français en Amérique', *Les Classiques de la colonisation*, Vol. I. Paris: Presses universitaires de France, 1946.

BIGGAR, H. P. 'The Early Trading Companies of New France', *Toronto University Studies in History and Economics*, Extra Vol. I, 1901.

—— ed. *The Voyages of Jacques Cartier*, Ottawa, 1924. *The Works of Samuel de Champlain*, 6 vols. Toronto: Champlain Society, 1922–26.

BISHOP, MORRIS. *Champlain, the Life of Fortitude*. London: Macdonald & Co., 1949.

BREBNER, J. B. *The Explorers of North America, 1492–1806*. 2nd ed. London: Black, A. & C., 1955.

BURPEE, L. J. ed. *Journals and Letters of Pierre Gaultier de Varennes de la Vérendrye.* Toronto: Champlain Society, 1927.

COLE, C. W. *Colbert and a Century of French Mercantilism.* 2 vols. New York: Columbia University Press, 1939.

GANONG, W. F. ed. *The Description and Natural History of the Coasts of North America.* Toronto: Champlain Society, 1908.

GRANT, W. L. and H. P. BIGGAR, eds. *The History of New France by Marc Lescarbot.* 3 vols. Toronto: Champlain Society, 1907–14.

INNIS, H. A. *The Fur Trade in Canada.* Revised ed. Toronto: University of Toronto Press, 1956.

NUTE, G. L. *Caesars of the Wilderness.* New York: D. Appleton-Century, 1943.

PARKMAN, F. *The Jesuits in North America in the Seventeenth Century,* any edition.

PRUD'HOMME, L.-A. 'Pierre Gaultier de Varennes, Sieur de la Vérendrye', *Proceedings and Transactions of the Royal Society of Canada,* 2nd ser., XI (1905), sec. I, 9–57.

—— 'Les Successeurs de la Vérendrye sous la domination française', *Proceedings and Transactions of the Royal Society of Canada,* 2nd ser., XII (1906), sec. I, 65–81.

II

THE AMERICAN FRONTIER

IN my first lecture I tried to give some idea of the French background to the Montreal fur trade, leading up to the position at 1763 and the loss of Canada to England. After 1763 the fur trade from Montreal spread westward in two main streams. The first ran up to Lake Huron and then either to Mackinac and Lake Michigan, or to Detroit and Lake Erie. In either case it led to the furs of the south and west, to Illinois, to the Miamis, and to the headwaters of the Missouri. The other stream also ran to Lake Huron, then past Sault Ste. Marie and along the north shore of Lake Superior to Kaministikwia, turning north from there by Pigeon River, Rainy Lake, Lake of the Woods, Lake Winnipeg, the Saskatchewan, and into the northwest. A southwest trade and a northwest trade had been developed from Montreal. Both used the Ottawa River route to get to Georgian Bay and Lake Huron, and both were dependent ultimately upon the mercantile competence of Montreal and upon the Atlantic shipping which connected Montreal to the markets of metropolitan France.

Of those two routes the southern was reinforced by an additional route, by way of Niagara and the Richelieu

River, which led behind the English colonies and increased the rivalry with the New England traders—who also profited by the fur trade when and as they could. But both of these routes, the southwest and the northwest, were in any case in commercial rivalry with the English: the southwest trade with the New England colonies and the northwest trade with the Hudson's Bay Company.

It is difficult to break down this trade into figures, but it is not impossible to get an impression of the balance between the northwest and the southwest trade; and it is worth while to do so at this juncture, at the end of the French régime, because it is important to realize that the later predominance of the northwest trade was scarcely observable in 1763. Among the trade returns in the Public Record Office there is no return for the actual year 1763, but for 1764 the returns are 106,000 skins from Canada as a whole; then as peace supervenes they rise in 1765 to more than double that, 275,000, going up again in 1766 to almost 350,000 skins. How much of this rapidly increasing trade came from the southwest, how much from the northwest? It is difficult to be certain; but in 1767 figures are available for Mackinac, and they show that of all the canoes which set forth from Mackinac in that year, eighty-four went to the southwest, thirty-seven to the northwest. The southwest canoes went to Lake Michigan, La Baie (Georgian Bay) and the Mississippi. The northwest canoes went to Lake Huron, Lake Superior itself, and to the northwest by way of Lake Superior. These figures only relate to the canoes from Mackinac, but it would seem that something like twice the quantity of trade goods went to the southwest compared with those which went to the northwest. At least it is clear, as one tries to get some impression of the trade when the British took over in 1763 and in subsequent years, that the southwest trade commanded priority over the northwest. This is a picture which it is difficult to accept in view of the later predominance of the northwest, but it gives a true notion of the relative values of the two trades at this time.

When Wolfe had died on the Heights of Abraham, and when Montreal had subsequently been captured and the peace negotiations were under way, we would expect the fur trade to be a prime consideration for the negotiators of the peace. But there can be very little doubt that the fur trade was not predominantly in the minds of the negotiators in 1763. Neither the British officials in America nor the American merchants who traded between England and North America had any serious influence upon the peace. There is no evidence that their views were either pushed or listened to. The only evidence on this subject, which I know of, is that the Hudson's Bay Company rather pathetically laid a claim against 'those enemies of all mankind', the French, for damages sustained in time of peace. The claim could not in any case be met; it amounted to about £100,000, for damages incurred over very nearly a hundred years' period, and it had no effect whatever upon the terms of the peace. Policy, as the peace negotiators got to work, was in fact dictated by a slightly academic British concept of imperialism, by the notions of imperial economy which were held at Westminster, rather than by the facts of the fur trade.

The theory of empire which determined the lines upon which the peace was negotiated was a theory which was best summarized by Lord Shelburne when he wrote at this time (Shelburne comes again later, and comes uttering different prophecies) that 'The possession of territory is but a secondary point and is now considered to be more or less valuable as it is subservient to the interests of commerce, which is now the great object of ambition.' New markets were being sought rather than new territory; and for Shelburne the new markets were of 'millions more consequence than all our other conquests'. This is a period (well before the revolt of the American colonies), in which there was a substantial revulsion of feeling against colonies of rule, colonies of conquest; colonies of commerce, markets, were required.

Although the term 'mercantilism' was not in general use until a generation after the conquest of Canada, and was then projected back by historians to classify and to condemn three centuries of economic thought, in fact it was at this time, towards the end of the eighteenth century, that imperial economic theory was taking on the colour of 'mercantilism', being dominated by merchants, for merchant interests. Markets for the rising manufacturing economy of an England which was running into the Industrial Revolution, and which was seeking markets, assume a new importance. It was at this time that mercantilism took on its peculiar meaning and the concepts of a British imperial economy became mercantilist, dominated by merchant thinking, by the seeking

for markets—a 'manufacturers' imperialism'. This was
the dogmatic line of thought which dictated the terms of
peace. Possession of territory was but a secondary point,
new markets were 'of millions more consequence than
all our other conquests'.

Translated into terms of North America, of the opportunities which the British victory provided, this meant
that British negotiators at the peace wished to create in
the middle west a vast market in which British traders
could dispose of British goods and British manufactures.
That concept tied in with the concept that the coastal
lands should be allocated to settlement and colonization,
and should produce (especially from the south) the sub-
tropical staple products which could not be got from
Europe and which the British economy needed. When
the general purpose was worked into a practicable pattern the whole scheme became embroiled in an intensely
interesting controversy known as the 'Canada versus
Guadaloupe' controversy.

In the course of the war not only had French Canada
fallen into the hands of the British, but the French West
Indian sugar-growing islands had also fallen to Britain;
and as the peace negotiations were beginning to be foreshadowed the serious choice before the British negotiators was how much to give back. The West Indian
Islands tied in with British trade concepts; they could
become a market for British manufactures, they absorbed slaves whom the British could ship from West
Africa, and they produced sugar which the British could
refine and manufacture and sell for currency upon the
markets of Europe. Canada could produce nothing but

furs; and Britain could already get furs from Hudson's Bay. So there were strong arguments in favour of keeping Guadeloupe and the other West Indian Islands, and handing back Canada to the French. Moreover, the British North American settlers had for generations been increasingly difficult to govern and to impress with the need to remain within the empire. The need to 'contain' the American colonies was therefore already fully recognized and can be traced through endless speeches and memoranda of this period. So the arguments for a balanced imperial economy, for 'containing' the American colonists and for maintaining the empire as it stood, on the whole pointed towards handing back Canada (or a substantial portion of Canada) to the French, and keeping Guadeloupe. The argument was carried on against very little geographical knowledge; and one official memorandum from Governor Murray in 1762 informed the Cabinet that it was 'impossible to ascertain exactly what part of North America the French styled Canada, no Chart or Map whatever having fallen into our Hands or Publick Record of any kind to show what they understood by it.'

In the middle of these doubts and difficulties Britain achieved a remarkable naval victory, when Rodney captured Martinique in 1762 and changed the situation. In 1760 Chatham had not known which way to turn. 'Some are for keeping Canada; some Guadeloupe. Who will tell me?' said Chatham. 'Who will tell me which I shall be hanged for not keeping?' With Rodney's victory his problem was to some extent solved. It appears that already he had decided to keep Canada and Newfoundland; but he had not yet announced this decision when Rodney gave him far more power than he had imagined, at one stage of the negotiations, would be at his disposal. Consequently it became possible for him and for his successor Bute, if they wished, to take both the whole of the French West Indies and the whole of Canada. In fact, what they decided to do was to take only what they called the Neutral Islands in the West Indies (four islands which had almost put the English West Indies out of the sugar business because they were so much better run) but to take Canada in its fullest possible connotation. It was impossible to tell exactly what the French understood by Canada, but the connotation which the British now adopted was one which would have surprised them. For Canada was held to extend all the way west to the Mississippi. This meant that when Britain took over Canada in 1763 it was a Canada which included the present American middle west, reaching down behind the New England colonies and stretching westward to the Mississippi.

But although, by a piece of opportunism during the peace negotiations when Rodney's victory placed the possibility in British hands, Britain had taken this vastly enlarged Canada, she then turned to the other aspects of imperialism and decided not to make these vast and fertile areas available for settlement, but to create there the market for British manufacturers which was an equally strong point in British beliefs and theories. The middle west, which had adventitiously fallen to Britain's lap at the peace negotiations, was to be kept as a reserve for Indians, as a fur-bearing area to which British

D

traders would have access but in which settlement was to be forbidden.

This was not a completely new policy. As early as 1759, when Pennsylvania had asked that settlers be allowed to spread beyond the Appalachian Mountains, that colony had been ordered by the Privy Council not to grant any land in or near territory which was occupied by or reserved to the Indians; and Washington himself, as a land-hungry Virginian, had been repulsed in his attempt to acquire land at the back of Virginia, in fulfilment of the same policy. Then, as the peace gave the great areas of the middle west into British control, British policy was set out in the terms of the proclamation which was enunciated on 7 October 1763. This specified that an Indian Reserve should be established between the Appalachians and the Mississippi, and that the Appalachians should be a western boundary 'beyond which our people should not at present be permitted to settle.' Within the Indian Reserve free access was to be given to all traders subject to their being given a government licence; and the proclamation was followed up by a plan for the management of Indian affairs, promulgated in 1764. Actually this plan for the management of Indian affairs never took effect because it aimed to set up two Indian Departments, each with a superintendent. These would be outside normal colonial government control; and the governors (not unnaturally, as has happened so many times in colonial history) insisted that their authority ought not to be undermined by independent Indian or Native authorities. So from 1764 onward there existed a vast Indian Reserve between the Appalachians and the Mississippi in which settlement was officially forbidden, but to which all traders officially had access, and in which no special arrangements had been made for managing Indian affairs.

The first result of this was Pontiac's rebellion. The Indians did not know to whom they owed loyalty and did not wish to owe loyalty to any European power merely as a consequence of European wars and treaties. They did not wish to see their lands allocated out by Europeans, and there is a famous passage attributed to the Chief of the Ojibwas, claiming the ownership of the soil for the Indians. 'Englishman,' he told Alexander Henry, 'although you have conquered the French, you have not conquered us. We are not your slaves. These lakes, these woods and mountains, were left to us by our ancestors. They are our inheritance; and we will part with them to none.' The great rebellion organized by Pontiac was ultimately put down by soldiery (Major Robert Rogers and his Rangers at Detroit). It was the first and most obvious result of the British policy; but it was only the most obvious result among many, for the whole frontier was a seething ferment of chaotic maladjustment.

Following on the heels of the British troops, the 'Old Subjects' of the King came up from the New England colonies, many of them serving in the army, others supplying and contracting for the army as it fought the French. Settlers, suppliers, eager and speculative contractors, they rapidly engaged in the fur trade of Montreal. There was certainly one such in Alexander Henry (the Elder), who had made his way to Detroit in time for Pontiac's rebellion, who just escaped with his life, and who left a first-hand account of the massacres and the brutality of the rebellion. Alexander Henry survived and in course of time became one of the wealthier citizens of Montreal. They were colourful characters, but these 'Old Subjects' who followed in the wake of the British army, and took advantage of the opening of the fur trade to all traders (subject to licence), were if anything more troublesome than the French. They spread from Montreal by the routes which the French had opened up, both to the northwest and to the southwest; and their influence was soon felt even in the Hudson's Bay territories. Right up at Moose, the Hudson's Bay trader was reporting that he was beset with 'Interlopers who will be more Destructive to our trade than the French was'. For, said he, 'the French were in a manner Settled, their Trade fixed, their Standard moderate and Themselves under particular regulations and restrictions, which I doubt is not the Case now.'

The characteristics of the Old Subjects who invaded the trade from Montreal assumed additional importance because England's statesmen, having negotiated a peace which gave control of the fur trade to the British, then realized that this was a valuable asset. They began to hope that the British merchant might 'well get a bigger share of the trade with the upper country on account of the easy conveyance of goods', and that this advantage would be improved by 'the superior diligence and application of The British Traders'. But the Old Subjects were not alone in the trade. The French 'New Subjects' remained; and they also had their defects. Many as were the complaints about the Old Subjects, it was at the same time said that the New Subjects (the Frenchmen who had lived with Indians, the old coureurs de bois, who were now patriotic Britons because they could get goods for their trade from Britain) were only to be distinguished from the Indians because they had a greater capacity for liquor and a greater propensity to vice.

Old and New Subjects alike would not have been engaged in the fur trade if they had been sober and responsible citizens. The official policy to control these unruly men was indeterminate and ineffective. Governor Murray had taken over the western lands with a well-justified suspicion of the merchants. His feeling, as he reported, was that 'few mercantile men will speak truths when inconsistent with self-interest.' Governor Carleton succeeded Murray with far greater confidence in the merchants, accepting their experience of the Indian frontier and listening to their opinions and advice. His attitude resulted in allowing the trade to develop, and this it did rapidly and extensively under Carleton.

As the British government favoured an expanding trade, the great rebellion of Pontiac obviously called for measures to garrison and police the Indian frontier. This led to the establishment of posts for garrisons; and in its turn it produced figures for the fur trade conducted at those posts. They were not very reliable figures, for they were produced in political debate, but they are informative in setting out the costs of Canada and the revenues to be derived from it. In fact, what happened

was that Great Britain tried (as she has tried on many
other occasions) to tell the colonists that, if they wished
to be defended, they must pay for their own defence. So
a tax was to be put upon the fur trade to pay for the
western garrisons. Inevitably this would have proved
impossible to collect, and in due course (and this is not
without significance) the tax upon the fur trade was
abandoned and a Stamp Tax was imposed to replace it
and to raise the necessary revenue for maintaining the
garrisons—garrisons which were necessary in the western posts largely in order to protect the fur traders.
The need for economy in administering the newly ac-
quired middle west ran parallel with the need to placate
the American colonists on the one hand, and to regu-
larize the fur trade on the other. A plan for unified control, for departmentalizing the fur trade, failed and was
abandoned in 1768. The commissioners appointed to
regulate Indian affairs under this system were recalled,
and the regulation of the fur trade was turned over to
the individual colonies—to Pennsylvania, New York,
Carolina, and, among others, Canada. The Indian Departments of those colonies, including that of Canada,
were given the duty of regulating the trade in such
fashion that incidents such as Pontiac's Rebellion should
not recur. Under this system, as the unified notion of a
midwestern fur trade was abandoned, Canada was given
the fur trade of the Great Lakes; and since New York,
which was supposed to be responsible for the fur trade of
Detroit, did not take up that responsibility and the fur
trade from that area actually came through Mackinac,
Montreal, and the Canadian route, Canada (without

specifically having this responsibility) took control of the trade of Detroit also. So from 1768 onward, as the plan for unified control of the fur trade was abandoned, Canada, controlling the trade of the Great Lakes and Detroit, had responsibility for both the southwest and the northwest branches of the trade which ran from Montreal.

Under this régime the fur trade expanded rapidly. The colonies were supposed 'to provide effectual laws to prevent settlements' and 'for the control and punishment of those attrocious Frauds and Abuses which have been practised by the Traders, and have been one principal cause of the Disaffection of the Savages'. In fact, they could do very little. The character of the traders, whether French New Subjects or American Old Subjects, dominated the trade. Governor Croghan of New York wrote that the French were 'an idle, lazy set, a parcel of renegades from Canada much worse than the Indians'. Governor Gage thought the French were better than the English and easier to call to account. 'For', said Governor Gage, 'the English ramble everywhere, they are generally of no Character, and desperate fortune.' English and French alike thought only of their immediate profit. The period of rapid expansion after 1768 was still marked by the highly suspect characters of those in the forefront of the trade and was therefore a period of heavy troubles, especially on the Ohio and on the Mississippi, where the trade was conducted with unscrupulous competition.

The southern trade did not attract all the attention. This was also a period of great growth in the trade of

Mackinac, the northern bastion of the western trade. It was a period in which payment for licences could not be enforced, and in which the outstanding men could not be easily controlled. Major Robert Rogers, for example, was placed in command of Mackinac, but he himself took to the trade, organizing the traders and supplying them. Rogers eventually had to be broken for treason and fraud, but he sent Johnathan Carver out to explore for the Western Sea, producing one of the famous travel books of this period and stimulating considerable interest in the fur trade and in Canada's western lands. Eventually Carver's *Travels through the interior parts of North America* played its part in stirring up the English to seek a route out to the west. Initially its importance lay in the revelation of the dangers of the Indian frontier at this time when the Indians, uneasy and ill-disciplined, were controlled by the separate colonies. Canada was responsible for much of this problem; but much also rested with the American colonies and the Treaty of Fort Stanwix in 1768 was merely an interlude (and not a particularly happy one) in this period.

In such circumstances the garrisons of the western forts became all-important, for the frontier was an uneasy one. It was reckoned that the cost of the garrisons amounted to £350,000 a year; but when in 1764 the proposed tax on the fur trade for this purpose was replaced by the Stamp Act, the American colonists took this as merely one more 'impertinent badge of slavery', a further revelation of English incompetence and of the English sense of superiority.

The Stamp Act, considered as a measure of frontier

policy, was followed by the Quebec Act of 1774. As the separate colonies proved incompetent to regulate their own fur trade, the feeling for a general unified policy became dominant once more. Quebec, New York, and Pennsylvania acted together in forbidding the sale of rum and in adopting a uniform system of taxes; but drunken Indians and licentious traders continued. 'Strollers', as they were called, promiscuous, unlicensed settlers, began to invade the Indian reserves and became an endless source of trouble. The Indians were constantly in revolt, while American settlers took advantage of the troubles (as always in colonial history) to proclaim that Indian rebellions cancelled out native rights; as, for example, when what came to be called Lord Dunmore's War opened the whole of Kentucky to settlement.

In this invasion of Indian lands there was a growing distinction between the northern and the southern fur trades. In the southern trade the fine furs were almost played out. Deer skins (and not always good deer skins) came to be more important in the south, while from about 1774 onward the fine pelts were coming more and more from the northwest, less and less from the southwest. The argument, therefore, that a vast hunting reserve should be maintained to absorb manufactured goods, and to produce furs in return, was losing out in the south to the argument of settlement. For it was to be expected that the settler would raise a numerous and ever-hungry family, and would produce a market for manufactured goods. Since a distinction between the northwest and southwest trade on these lines developed at the same time as the need for a unified and effective policy came to be felt, it was Canada and the northwest trade which assumed paramount importance. This was the situation which the Quebec Act of 1774 tackled by putting the government of Quebec, the law of Quebec, and the courts of justice of Quebec into the position of responsibility for the fur traders in Canada. Canada, so defined, meant the whole of Canada as accepted in 1763, extending through the midwest to the Mississippi.

Like the Stamp Act, the Quebec Act was designed for the fur-trade frontier. But it was also taken by the American colonies as a deliberate affront to them, taking from their colonial control, and putting under Canadian control, vast areas which were potential settlement land. The Act was also regarded, quite inevitably, as a retrograde step, extending French law, the French language, Roman Catholicism, and the fur trade of Montreal into territories which could be, and in part were, supplied through Boston, New York, Albany, and the middle west. The Quebec Act moreover, although framed before the Boston Tea Party, was held to be a deliberate affront inflicted because of the Boston rising. The avowed purpose of this act was to go back to the point at which the British had come into the middle west, to reassert the frontier policy of forbidding settlement and of creating an Indian reserve from which furs could be taken, and into which manufactured goods could be sold. Such explanations are, today, valid and reasonable. In 1774 they were not acceptable. The Quebec Act caused endless discontent and was one definite cause of the rising tide of hostility from the North American colonists.

In fact, the Quebec Act was followed closely by the outbreak of war. During the war, strangely enough, the northwest trade increased rapidly because access to England and supplies of goods continued, whereas the United States were fought over, were cut off from European supplies and cut off from European markets. Montreal was very little affected although the Americans marched northwards and captured it. Trade continued; and as soon as the war was over trade expanded even more. The southwest trade, even of Montreal, was more seriously affected than the northwest, for it was upset by the restriction of navigation on the Great Lakes and by the American shortage of goods. Yet as the war drew to a conclusion, the fur trade of Montreal was undoubtedly expanding. From Canada in 1782, the last year of the war, there were 120 canoes and 250 batteaux worth about £184,000 licenced for the Indian trade; in the next year, 126 canoes and 321 batteaux worth almost £227,000, a significant increase in which batteaux rather than canoes, and heavy goods which suited batteaux, counted enormously.

This was the situation when Britain came to negotiate the definition of the American frontier, the subject of this lecture. Now if the Treaty of 1763, by which she took over Canada, was a very odd treaty from many points of view, the Treaty of 1783 by which she accepted the independence of the Americans, was still more odd. Here I would quote from two American historians, Morrison and Commager, to support the view that the terms of the treaty were not the result of the military situation as the war dragged to an end, but of other considerations. What they say is this: 'Considering that the British still held New York, Charleston, Savannah, and seven posts in the Northwest, that Washington's army was almost incapable of further effort, and the British navy commanded the seas, it is surprising what wide boundaries and favourable terms the United States obtained.' In fact, the treaty was very largely negotiated by Lord Shelburne (whom I have mentioned already). Between the acquisition of Canada and the loss of America, Shelburne had changed his views in one important respect. He had moved from not desiring to acquire territories into desiring to get rid of them. This was a decisive step. He was convinced that there was no possibility of effectively governing the American colonies, and that the object of the British government therefore should be to part with them on such terms that they would remain friendly and that they would remain good customers.

In trying to achieve this object (like so many British colonial negotiators since) Shelburne bypassed the ordinary channels of diplomatic communication and employed an amateur diplomat, a determined idealist, of his own choosing. The negotiations were conducted in Paris by Richard Oswald. Richard Oswald was a London merchant who, through his wife, owned very considerable American estates and was a business associate of Henry Laurens, one of the American commissioners. He was noted for his candour and his appreciation of American views, and was usually ahead of the Americans, anticipating their demands. It is not surprising that the conduct of these negotiations, which resulted in the setting up of the independent United States of America, is one of the most astonishing chapters in British diplomatic and imperial history. Oswald himself was a transparently honest man, and an idealist. His reports, it has been said, are a wilderness of prolixity; but they have the advantage that they give a first-hand, day-to-day commentary on what actually took place. He represented the advanced group who looked forward to independence, and to the achievement of that independence on terms that would leave the minimum imperial responsibility with Great Britain. For him Canada, as well as the American colonies, should be signed away. But even Shelburne turned down Oswald's suggestion that the United States ought to have Canada. This was a suggestion put forward by Franklin; although supported by Oswald, it was turned down not only by Shelburne, but by George III, by Townsend, and by the other British negotiators.

In the initial stages, the British also rejected the claim that America should take the midwestern territory which had fallen to Britain in 1763. This would have given America the lands right through to the Mississippi, and the preliminary discussions of 1782, which took place in Paris, insisted upon the frontier as before the Quebec Act, which had placed these lands under Canadian control. In the subsequent negotiations, although there were no good maps available and there was very little care for the fur trade as such, there was also a predominant desire to make a peace which would leave an atmosphere of 'good neighbourliness'. But Haldimand, as Governor of Canada, wished to retain Niagara and Oswego for military reasons; and from about 1780 onward the Montreal fur traders had begun to lobby in London.

During the twenty years between 1763 and 1783 the Montreal traders had become very wealthy and important people, commanding both the southwest and the northwest trade, and profiting from both. It was James McGill who estimated (in a memorial to the Board of Trade) that Montreal's trade ran at about £180,000 a year, of which £100,000 came from south of the boundary which was then under discussion. The figures available for the fur trade in 1780–85 were highly suspect, for they were all produced with a particular result in view. Shelburne reckoned that Canada cost about £800,000 a year to defend and that the import trade was only worth £50,000 a year. These were wildly improbable figures. In fact the trade ran at about a quarter of a million pounds a year, plus or minus. But this was still an important trade, from any point of view; and it entitled the Montreal merchants to a hearing in London. They can be found there, in groups of two, or three, or seven at a time, pressing their case and advocating retention of the western lands and maintenance of British garrisons in the western posts. But when the tortuous negotiations in Paris resulted in the treaty signed on 3 September 1783, the terms of that treaty were not dictated by the needs of the fur traders any more than they were dictated by the realities of the military situation. The treaty was signed because the Americans were frightened that the French, their allies, would sacrifice them in order to get concessions in Canada, while the British were afraid that the French would stand firm on the American side in order to be revenged for the loss of Canada. Shelburne's ministry had fallen and the Fox-North Coalition was conducting the negotiations—a coalition mistrusted by the country and hated by the king. These were not ideal conditions in which to negotiate what proved to be one of the most important peace treaties of modern history—a treaty which placed upon the map the United States of America. That treaty was negotiated in conditions of precipitancy, lack of confidence, lack of knowledge; and the last factor becomes increasingly apparent when the frontier of the new republic is considered.

The treaty took the St. Lawrence as the frontier, drawing the line through the middle of the St. Lawrence and through the middle of the Great Lakes up to Pigeon River on the north shore of Lake Superior. The mouth of Pigeon River was the point at which Kaministikwia had been founded as the great entrepôt from which the northwest trade branched off; alongside Pigeon River lay the Grand Portage, the route out from the Great Lakes, over the Height of Land to Rainy Lake and the northwest trade. So a frontier running through the Great Lakes to Pigeon River, and then up the river to the northwest angle of Lake of the Woods, and so along the forty-ninth parallel to the headwaters of the Mississippi, would at its best be taking the fur-trade route as the boundary line, and might well throw that route into American hands. For the moment these problems were left unsettled. There were endless discussions of free navigation of the waterways, of taxes on the fur trade, of equal access for nationals of both countries to the territory which was given to the United States. All those questions were left to be settled by a subsequent treaty. In 1783 there was no time to reach a conclusion; some sort of treaty had to be signed in a hurry, because nobody trusted France and because the Fox-North Coalition was tottering. The result has been condemned as 'the shameful terms of peace'; and the terms were shameful not because they acknowledged American independence, but because they gave the middle west to the United States. These were millions of miles of fertile territory in which the axe of the American settler had never yet rung; they had only been opened up by the fur trader from Montreal.

As yet there were no maps available to underline the defects of the treaty. But as the territory came to be known, the Pigeon River frontier proved to be only one defect among many. Other defects were, first of all, that the forty-ninth parallel running westward from the northwest corner of Lake of the Woods never got to the Mississippi, for the sources of that river lay to the south of such a line and the river did not run that way. Second, the Grand Portage was absolutely essential for the northwest trade. It lay in American territory, six miles on the wrong side of the frontier. Third, the treaty placed the south shore of Lake Superior in American hands and the north shore was bleak and inhospitable for three hundred miles. It was difficult and almost impossible to get craft up Sault Ste. Marie into Lake Superior unless the south shore could be used. So at two points the Montreal fur trade was cut off from essential means of transportation, at the Grand Portage and on the south shore of Sault Ste. Marie; and at one point it was alleged to have access to the Mississippi, with free navigation to be settled by subsequent commercial treaty, whereas the Mississippi lay entirely to the south of the boundary.

As these defects came to be appreciated, the saving feature of the treaty was that the precise definition of the boundary was left open, to be settled by a later treaty. In the meantime British garrisons remained in the posts of the west. This was another open question, left to be settled later; for the treaty said that the garrisons should be vacated 'with all convenient speed'. Such a phrase is, of course, almost meaningless; and when peace had been achieved the British garrisons were not withdrawn and the Montreal fur traders continued their trade. Not only did Governor Haldimand (considerably influenced by the fur merchants) retain British garrisons in the posts, he turned back with ignominy an American military mission which came up under General Steuben to take them over. It was not yet 'convenient' to withdraw.

During the interval between the signing of the peace treaty in 1783 and the subsequent settlement of the outstanding problems in 1794, British merchants, especially the great Montrealers, settled down to enjoy their opportunity to use Kaministikwia as a depot, and to use the Grand Portage as a route to carry their trade up to the Winnipeg drainage area, and so up the Saskatchewan, ultimately to the Arctic, and over the Rockies to the Pacific. This was a magnificent period for the Montreal fur trader, and Montreal rose with impressive

E

speed to outstanding stature. This was the growth period of the Northwest Company, and the period came to an end as far as the American frontier was concerned when the Americans began to insist that the garrisons should be withdrawn. Discussions between Hammond, British Minister in Washington, and Jefferson were prompted by the Montrealers' suggestions for adjusting the boundary and yielding the Grand Portage to the Canadians. But the Americans refused to consider separate issues and pressed for a comprehensive solution of all outstanding problems, including the western posts. When the garrisons were withdrawn then, as part of a comprehensive treaty, they would settle the other problems.

The Americans in the meantime were getting the measure of their Indian problem, and in 1794 General Wayne broke the power of the tribes of the northwest at Fallen Timbers and gave the Americans effective control of the middle west. Then John Jay was sent to London to settle outstanding differences. As part of the settlement the British agreed to surrender all the posts south of the lakes and to evacuate them. The British garrisons were to be withdrawn, definitely, by the first of June 1796. In the territory south of the lakes trade was to be free both to Canadians and to Americans, the rivers and the portages were to be open to navigation by both; so was the Mississippi. But as yet none knew where the Mississippi rose nor how its headwaters ran in relation to the boundary. No discriminatory duties were to be placed on the trade of either side. But the fur trade of this southwestern area was a declining asset; and so, as

Jay's Treaty came to be signed in November 1794, and the Americans took possession of the posts south of the lakes, they took possession of an area which (for commercial reasons as distinct from political considerations) had very largely run through its fur-bearing animals—an area in which the Montreal fur traders had almost (but not quite) lost interest. There was indeed still a considerable trade in peltry, but it was largely in deer skins; and settlement had come to be more important than trade, and more a matter of policy. The English policy of a great reserve for the fur trade had been specifically abandoned.

The division of territory foreshadowed in 1783 and specified in detail in Jay's Treaty ran along the division with which I started this lecture. So the natural geographical division between the northwest trade and the southwest trade became a division marked also by the American frontier. As that happened, the wealthy, politically and diplomatically important fur traders in Montreal were faced with a decision. They had grown to great stature by supporting British armies, by supplying British garrisons, by endless lobbying of British politicians and governors and soldiers. Now they must either become American citizens if they wished to continue with the southwest trade, or they must remain Montrealers, New Subjects or Old Subjects according to their origins, if they wished to continue in the northwest trade through Kaministikwia and the Grand Portage. But they would have to find some other way of getting into that northwest trade, because the Grand Portage now lay on the wrong side of the American frontier.

Concentration on the northern trade, and development of routes and a supply system appropriate for that trade, is what the Northwest Company achieved. It was an achievement in which the vigorous and colourful personalities of the members of that company count for much, but of which the value depends upon an appreciation of the geographical factors which were involved.

Suggestions for further reading:

ALVORD, C. W. 'Lord Shelburne and the Founding of British-American Goodwill', *Proceedings of the British Academy*. London: Oxford University Press, 1926.

BAIN, J. ed. *Travels and Adventures in Canada and the Indian Territories . . . by Alexander Henry*. Toronto: 1901.

CARVER, JONATHAN. *Travels through the Interior Parts of North America, 1766–68*. London, 1781.

GIPSON, L. H. *The Coming of the Revolution, 1763–1775*. The New American Nation Series. New York, 1954.

GRANT, S. L. 'Canada versus Guadeloupe', *American Historical Review*, XVII (July 1912), 735–93.

HARLOW, V. T. *The Founding of the Second British Empire, 1763–93*, Vol. I. London: Longmans, 1952.

JOHNSON, SIR W. *The Papers of Sir William Johnson*, edited by James Sullivan and A. C. Flick. 10 vols. Albany: The University of the State of New York, 1921–62.

KELLOGG, L. P. *The French Régime in Wisconsin and the Northwest*. Madison: State Historical Society of Wisconsin, 1925.

MASSON, L. F. R. *Les Bourgeois de la compagnie du nord-ouest*. 2 vols. Québec: A. Coté, 1889–90.

MORISON, S. E. and H. S. COMMAGER. *The Growth of the American Republic*. 2 vols. 5th ed. New York: Oxford University Press, 1962.

PARKMAN, F. *The Conspiracy of Pontiac*. 2 vols. New York: Dutton, 1910.

PHILLIPS, P. C. *The Fur Trade*. 2 vols. Norman, Oklahoma: University of Oklahoma Press, 1961.

REID, M. G. 'The Quebec Fur-Traders and Western Policy, 1763–1774', *Canadian Historical Review*, VI (March 1925), 15–32.

WALLACE, W. S. 'The Pedlars from Quebec', *Canadian Historical Review*, XIII (December 1932), 387–402.

III

THE NORTHWEST COMPANY

THE fur trade which had been developed by the French from Montreal, whether it ran to the Great Lakes and southwest to Detroit, the Illinois, the Miamis, and the headwaters of the Missouri, or from Lake Superior by the Grand Portage to Lake Winnipeg, the Saskatchewan, and the northwest, was in either case largely taken over by the Old Subjects of the Crown who followed the British armies to Montreal. Their rapidly expanding trade was deeply concerned at the conclusion of the American War of Independence, when the American frontier posed problems of access to Lake Superior (if the southern shore went to the United States) and problems of break-out from Lake Superior to the northwest (if Pigeon River and the Grand Portage should lie within the American frontier). But although these problems drove the Montreal traders to the formation of significant groups and syndicates so as to formulate and to press their views, the actual fur trade was but little affected until Jay's Treaty of 1794. For although the American Treaty was made in a great hurry, with very little geographical knowledge and very little consideration for the fur trade as such, nevertheless a ten-year period elapsed during which the British traders had possession of the western posts—and during which they fully exploited that advantage.

The Old Subjects of the Crown, who took over the Montreal fur trade during the period from about 1763 to about 1794, were sometimes settlers from the American colonies who had followed the British troops north. But a second influx of such colonials came during the American War of Independence, particularly when the Americans took Montreal. When Jay's Treaty set out the frontier of America and made it clear that henceforth the southwest trade would lie in the hands of American citizens, and that the northwest trade had to find some way around the American possession of the Grand Portage, the trade from Montreal had been almost completely taken over by such Old Subjects. Enterprise, rather than any legal discrimination, had given them mastery over the French New Subjects who had conducted the trade twenty years previously. There were indeed numbers of New Subjects still engaged in the trade, but they figured predominantly as Indian traders and canoe masters, not as merchants and owners of warehouses. The role of the merchants controlling and directing the trade was almost entirely taken up by the Old Subjects.

These new Montrealers were often remarkably virile personalities. To go through them biographically would be exhausting; but one or two should illustrate the kind of person with whom we are dealing. First comes Simon McTavish, born in Scotland in 1750, emigrating with his elder sister and her husband to New York at the age of thirteen, just at the time that the French provinces fell into British hands. McTavish served an apprenticeship in New York and then came north, and by 1770 was engaged in transporting rum from Albany to the Montreal traders. He moved into Montreal as a resident in 1774, just before the Americans captured the city, and he stayed on when the American tide had receded. Though he does not appear to have participated actively in the fur trade until 1775, when he traded to the southwest, he was taking a cargo of furs worth £15,000 to the United Kingdom in 1776. McTavish was primarily a merchant, an organizer who never went beyond the Grand Portage (but the Grand Portage was a two-months' journey from Montreal, and this is not to be held against him), a man of fine tastes, with a fondness for oysters, pretty girls, and extravagant living. He was known, significantly, in the fur trade as the Marquis. Against McTavish might be set any number of more vigorous, active traders—of whom the brothers Frobisher are as representative as any. These were three dour Yorkshiremen, who also came up to Montreal from the American colonies. But, unlike McTavish, they had themselves ventured right up the Saskatchewan, to the foot of the Rockies and over the Height of Land to Athabaska and the Mackenzie drainage basin. But although they were tough wintering traders they proved if anything tougher and more truculent when they gave up wintering and returned to Montreal to become merchants. Ultimately they went into partnership with Simon McTavish, described themselves as directors and principals of the concern and were the sort of men who, when offered a deal by a rival, laconically replied that the 'sun shined for everybody and they must make the most of their chances'. In contrast with the 'fine Italian hand' of McTavish, the Frobishers appear as uncompromising, truculent, hard-working, and hard-headed Yorkshiremen—which they were. In their sturdiness and in their surliness they are a necessary part of any attempt to assess the Montreal traders.

But perhaps the best individual example of the Old Subjects who took over the Montreal fur trade was Peter Pond—a New Englander who had joined the army and had risen to commissioned rank by the time of the siege of Montreal, when he was but twenty years old. His career was marked throughout by a capacity for purposeful thought and by even more purposeful action. Pond was suspected, with good reason, of three murders during his career; and though none of them was ever judicially brought home to him there can be little doubt that his was a character capable of such action. When he embarked upon the fur trade he ventured first from Montreal to Mackinac and then down to Detroit and the Mississippi. He made his first success in the southwest trade, as McTavish had done, and he then turned to the northwest. Here he was more responsible than any other single person for the planned and organized expansion of the trade from the Grand Portage northwestward. We shall come across Peter Pond again; he was particularly important because he drove the outfitting depots forward in order that the wintering traders could penetrate farther and farther into the fur-bearing territories.

These are a very few of the striking personalities who took over the Montreal fur trade. Because of the strength of their characters and the liveliness of the biographical records, the history of the Northwest Company has come to be written largely in terms of personalities and of amalgamations, syndicates, and companies which depend upon personalities, friendships, and animosities. The basic geographical factors which conditioned the entire development of the Montreal fur trade tend to be overlooked. But when all allowances have been made for the business acumen, the knowledge, and the driving power which these men brought to the fur trade, it must be emphasized that they brought these faculties to bear upon opportunities as they occurred; and that such opportunities must be analysed and understood in geographical terms. Groups, syndicates, combinations, and companies are of course personal arrangements. In the fur trade of Montreal they were formed to exploit geographical situations; and changes in the groupings must be linked to geographical knowledge, theory, or opportunity.

Before the actual cession of the land to the British in 1761, the first recorded combination among the traders significantly called itself la Société du Nordouest. This was a combination of Forrest Oakes, James Stanley, and William Grant; and its function was to act as merchant outfitters, sharing the cost of sending out a French coureur de bois, De la Fleur, on a trading expedition to Detroit. There, like Alexander Henry, De la Fleur got involved in the Conspiracy of Pontiac; but he also survived. The Société du Nordouest is merely one example of one type of combination of which there were clearly many variants. In 1766 there is evidence of an arrangement which is perhaps of more importance, since it involved the great trader Alexander Henry himself. He also made a combination with a French coureur, J.-B. Cadotte, sending him out to Fond du Lac and making a great deal of money from the venture. Many of these early syndicates took this form, with English merchants outfitting French coureurs to take canoe-loads of goods up to the pays d'en haut. They still often went to the southwest trade rather than to the northwest, and the drive which was generated by such combinations caused Governor Murray to complain of the 'licentious fanaticks who are trading here'.

Such combinations were due to the desire to exploit the possibilities which were opened up as the cession of Canada placed the trade of the west in British hands; and, since it was a trade of French origin which was being exploited, it is not surprising that the combinations often took a form in which a British merchant could utilize a French coureur's ability to travel and to trade with Indians.

The opportunities offered by the temporary arrangements for the western lands were obviously precarious. Government policy regarding the Indian reservation and the fur trade of the west was uncertain and subject to constant discussion; and it was almost inevitable that the fur traders should organize themselves so as to bring their knowledge and their interest to bear upon the politicians. As they spread their trade over the land, and as they became more wealthy and influential, they also organized in order to achieve their common interests. They briefed a London solicitor, Fowler Walker, to plead their case when the terms for the cession of Canada were under discussion, and they submitted the 'Memorial of the Merchants of Montreal' of 1766. The purpose of this memorial was to secure free exploitation of the western trade and to protest against Governor Murray's confining the trade to fortified posts. The signatures give a good indication of the way in which the British merchants had moved into a controlling position by 1766, for the memorandum was signed by Isaac Todd, Forrest Oakes, Richard Dobie (the greatest merchant of Montreal), James Finlay, and Benjamin Frobisher; the list is not exhaustive, and it would be easy to add to it such names as Alexander Henry, the McGills, the other two Frobisher brothers, or Simon McTavish (who was on his voyage to England at that time). But the signatories of this memorial clearly represent a powerful and co-ordinated group of forceful and reputable merchants.

Against the background of the opportunities offered by the cession of Canada, the Montreal merchants made their temporary alliances, they outfitted traders and they lobbied interminably, in London as in Quebec. They undoubtedly exercised considerable influence on the higher policy of the fur-trade frontier; and, as the run of the trade began to turn northwest rather than southwest, so did the interests of the syndicates. In 1769 a more lasting alliance was made when Isaac Todd and James McGill joined with the three Frobisher brothers and sent an expedition up to Rainy Lake and into the Lake Winnipeg area. Again, they were not alone in trading into this area; but the syndicates seldom lasted for more than one or two years. It is possible to get an insight into the sort of arrangements which were being made when, in 1771, one of the *voyageurs* who was employed by such a syndicate deserted to the Hudson's Bay people and described the system to them. It appeared that at Cedar Lake, at the outlet of the Saskatchewan, a 'Pedlar' called Thomas Corry had established himself— a rumbustious trader who expected the Hudson's Bay men to enter into trade with him but who wrote to tell them that the Indian upon whom they most relied would not be coming down to the Bay because he had 'Drunk so much Brandy this winter he Canot Come'. Corry and his drunken Indians were in a strategic position at Cedar Lake, and the deserter John Cole showed that he had a strong and flexible organization behind him. He had been outfitted for his voyage from Mackinac to Cedar Lake by a partnership which traded at Mackinac and which consisted of Isaac Todd, George McBeath, and Corry himself. This partnership in turn had been supplied by a Montreal firm which consisted of a pair of brothers, Blondeau and Keshew (an example of French New Subjects continuing as merchants), who themselves had been supplied by John Walker at Quebec.

Behind these Canadian merchants were ranged about eight London supply houses who, year by year, shipped out an assortment of goods for the Indian trade to their agents and customers at Quebec or Montreal. The Quebec and Montreal merchants took the consignments over and distributed the goods to the Montreal traders, who made up their own consignments and sent them up to the supply depots at Detroit or Mackinac. There other groups of merchants took over the goods and fitted out the coureurs de bois, the 'pedlars' as the Hudson's Bay men called them, who actually went out and traded with the Indians. This was a pattern within which there was infinite variety. For example, Thomas Corry figures as a pedlar on the Saskatchewan, but he also appears as a merchant at Mackinac. Similarly Blondeau appears as a merchant at Montreal, but he was also an outstanding Indian trader on the Upper Saskatchewan. Sometimes such traders were independent, sometimes they worked on commission, sometimes they were plain employees; but within the variations the one constant and outstanding feature was that the whole system was run on credit. The London merchants supplied the goods on credit, the Quebec and Montreal merchants took them over on credit and shipped them upcountry on credit, and the Indian traders took their outfits on credit and supplied their Indians with advances on credit. The whole system therefore, being tied to credit, was dependent upon detailed and accurate accounts, or upon high profits to offset slipshod accountancy. As is the way of credit-trade, it produced great profits on some occasions —and even greater losses on others.

While this is a picture of the developments which were occurring in the lower country, in the northwest other combinations were taking place for other reasons —reasons which were even more cogently geographical. For the 'fanaticks', of whom Governor Murray complained, were pushing the trade farther and farther afield in cutthroat competition with each other; and combinations which would enable resources to be pooled and the supply depot for traders to be established nearer to the trade area than Mackinac had a great appeal. These considerations applied particularly to traders on the Saskatchewan, which since Vérendrye had become the route by which Montreal traders penetrated into the northwest. There rivalry was indeed keen; but only experienced traders could get so far, and, being experienced and having spent their winters alongside each other in outspoken but not unfriendly rivalry, they found no difficulty in entering into upcountry combinations which repeated many of the features of the syndicates of the merchants down below at the outfitting bases.

One of the most important of these trading combinations falls into the context of the Quebec Act of 1774 and the placing of responsibility for the trade of the whole of Canada with the authorities of Quebec. In 1775 a combination was formed consisting of James McGill, Benjamin Frobisher, Maurice Blondeau, and Alexander Henry. They all had experience as active Indian traders and they all had outstanding positions and prestige as Montreal merchants. Their purpose on this occasion was to take out a combined licence for trade on the Saskatchewan for one year, so that they could push their trade farther forward in opposition to the Hudson's Bay post at Cumberland House. Putting their canoes together and pooling their resources, they produced the most effective syndicate as yet seen on the Saskatchewan; in the next year, having made their initial impact on the Cumberland House trade, they used their organization to overcome the great geographical obstacle from which they suffered—the distance of Montreal from the active fur posts. In 1776 they shifted their supply base forward from Mackinac to Grand Portage, thereby saving their traders valuable time and making it possible for them to push their trade farther inland. These men, despite their Montreal connections, figure in this affair as traders on the Saskatchewan, and they were probably dependent for the Montreal aspects of their arrangement on Simon McTavish; for it was probably he who supplied their outfit and sent it up to Grand Portage for them.

So in 1775 the desire to penetrate farther up the Saskatchewan, especially in rivalry with the Hudson's Bay Company, led first to the formation of a syndicate of active traders, secondly to the moving forward of their supply base, and thirdly to integration of these forward traders with merchant houses in Montreal—whether it was Simon McTavish who forwarded their goods to Grand Portage for them or some other merchant. The circumstances of the trade demanded such action, both to overcome the distance involved and to challenge the trade of the Hudson's Bay Company; the years 1775 and 1776 saw great developments, and the Hudson's Bay men were told that the pedlars were all in one general concern. At Cumberland they were 'warned' in a general letter under the joint signatures of seven of the pedlars. The 'saucy pride' of one of the pedlars, William Holmes, merely elicited from the Hudson's Bay factor the rejoinder that 'Scotchmen can kill as well as Irishmen can'. But there can be no doubt that in the highly competitive and uneasy situation on the Upper Saskatchewan there were great advantages to be derived from the formation of such loose syndicates. In fact, they enabled the Montreal merchants to expand their trade rapidly and purposefully. In their shifting groups the pedlars spilled from the Saskatchewan basin over Portage la Loche into the Churchill River basin, and so into the Hudson's Bay territory, setting up their posts at Beaver Lake and at Ile-à-la-Crosse. As a result of moving their supply base forward in 1776–77 they had opened up a whole new fur-trading area. Then, in the following year, Peter Pond carried expansion a step further. He not only went over Portage la Loche to trade down Sturgeonweir River, but when he came out in the summer of 1778 he did not even go right down to the Grand Portage. He stayed on the Upper Saskatchewan and outfitted himself for the next winter from the unused 'remains' of trade goods which other traders had available there. Such an arrangement was of course completely dependent upon pooled resources, and the syndicate so formed enabled Pond to start off for his next venture at a very considerable advantage over any rival.

In 1778, therefore, Pond, with the great asset of a syndicate of partners who had equipped him from a temporary advanced forward base, was able to push his trade down to Clearwater River and almost to Lake Athabaska itself. He came out in 1779, having traded the very clothes off his back. He had realized the fur trader's dream, making his way past the trading Indians and reaching to unspoiled hunting Indians in magnifi-

F

cent fur-bearing country. Although he brought over eighty thousand fine beaver skins, he had traded still more which he was unable to bring with him, and from 1779–80 onwards Athabaska became the El Dorado of the fur trade, the scene towards which the efforts of the Montreal merchants were directed.

Peter Pond came right down to Montreal in 1779 after this epoch-making achievement; and there he found that a comprehensive reshuffle of the trading partnerships was taking place. He brought considerable experience of syndicates, and he brought unmistakeable evidence of the rich rewards which co-operation could bring. The lessons of the need for an advanced supply base, and of a stable syndicate to organize such a system, came most appropriately; for at Montreal a powerful group of Saskatchewan traders—the Frobisher brothers and Alexander Henry—were putting their resources together for precisely this purpose. Pond arrived in time to take part in the formation of the Northwest Company, officially so called.

For the Northwest Company, as it was set up in 1779, brought together seven smaller partnerships and two individual merchants. McTavish and Small, the Frobishers, Patterson and John McGill, Todd and James McGill, Holmes and Grant, Wadden and St. Germain (a Swiss and a French Canadian), and McBeath who also acted for Pond; these were the partnerships. The individual traders included were John Ross and Forrest Oakes. They all agreed to trade as a combined concern in order to facilitate the forwarding of goods for the northwest trade (which had been held up that year by delays in issuing licences), just as the need to get the supply depot forward had been underlined by Pond; and they agreed to trade in common, dividing their trade into sixteen shares, of which two would go to each of the partnerships and one each to the two individuals. This may seem a crude and almost impracticable sort of partnership, in which many details would require specification. But behind it lay considerable experience in the working of such combinations; and it must have been the result of prolonged discussion. The pooling of resources and the allocation of shares would be comparatively simple matters when considered in the light of licenced canoes, each of which would represent an 'interest' in the concern and the contribution of a particular member.

In fact, the strength and the weakness of the Northwest Company throughout its career do not seem to have stemmed from legal niceties in drafting the forms of agreement which bound the company together. For from the start, in 1779, it was never a company in the strict legal sense which would have made it a corporate unit in the eyes of the law, responsible for its debts, accountable for its actions, and capable of being sued as a single body. Rather it was a copartnership (as it was sometimes described), within which individual partners took action for the common interest. But the copartnership did not absorb all the activities of its members; they traded outside the Company as well as within it; and the copartnership worked with a good deal of rivalry and with signs of a struggle for power controlled by an agreement with definite limitations, which would run for a specified number of years. The Company's great opponent, Lord Selkirk, later claimed that it was so organized that it could 'wield the force of thousands of men, while it is scarcely possible to fix responsibility upon an individual partner possessed of funds in the concern'; and this was true of it at any time. But its lack of corporate responsibility was no bar to effective joint action by the partners, whether in organizing the details of their merchandising or in seeking and securing privileges. In the first year of its formation the Company brought the combined weight of the partners to support a powerful petition to Governor Haldimand, requesting passes; and the reshufflings which followed did not in any way derogate from the Company's importance or activity in such matters.

In fact, the partners being what they were, this great initial combination of the Northwest Company lasted for only one year—for with justice it was said that 'the parties seemed less anxious to fulfill it while it lasted than to prepare for its dissolution.' So, although the 'nine-parties agreement' was renewed at the end of its first year, it was quickly revised. The new agreement was intended to run for three years (from 1780 to 1783) though in fact it was abandoned after two years; again the joint trade was to be divided into sixteen shares; again the copartnership included many of the great merchants and some of the lesser men; and again many were left out. The resources of the new organization were mobilized to send Peter Pond into Athabaska in 1781. With the great houses of the Frobishers, McTavish, the McGills, and Ellice outfitting him, he was able to start for his winter trade from the Grand Portage. This, it is true, was not half-way up the Saskatchewan. But it was on the far side of Lake Superior, and the arrangement started Pond off as the most advanced trader of the Northwest Company with a great advantage over any rival.

There were, however, rivals afield, and some of them managed to get as far into the northwest as Pond, with all his advantages. Etienne Wadden, the Swiss who had been included in the partnership of 1779 with his French partner St. Germain but who was excluded by the arrangement of 1780, actually wintered alongside Pond at Lac la Ronge; and in the spring of 1782 the two men got into a quarrel. Wadden was killed. What happened has never been satisfactorily ascertained, but Pond was later acquitted of a charge of murder. The evidence, nevertheless, was strongly against him, and the malodour of the affair certainly played some part in breaking up the Northwest Company in 1782. But other partnerships were quickly formed, for the dynamic of the forward-moving fur-trade frontier was strong, and the logic of the argument for co-ordinated effort compelling.

The value of such partnerships was of course not confined to the northwest trade. In the southwest trade also they were equally appropriate; and in 1785 a General Company of Lake Superior and the South arose in parallel with the Northwest Company. The partners were Isaac Todd, the brothers McGill, and Charles Patterson. Their object was to exploit the opportunities offered at the end of the American War of Independence, as the western frontier and the possession of the posts were (at least for the time being) left in British hands. But Athabaska was rapidly becoming 'the vast extent of country from which the N. W. Co. may be said to draw their treasures', and, although other combinations were still in existence, there were particularly cogent reasons why the Northwest Company should renew a partnership which had proved necessary for trade to that region.

The Company therefore took on a new existence with an agreement which was hammered out during the winter of 1783–84. This was the time when the terms of the peace with the United States made it clear that there would need to be serious differences of approach between traders to the northwest and traders to the southwest, since the latter trade would lie to territory which would, at least officially, be American. Some of the original members of the Northwest Company (of 1779) therefore concentrated their attention on the southwest trade—and even formed a separate company for that purpose. For those merchants who decided to continue in the northwest trade, the American peace made it clear that there remained a limited period in which to do two things. First, they must try to find an alternative route to the Grand Portage in case it should in the end be taken from them; and second, they must bring pressure to bear to keep the Portage in British hands. The re-formed Company set about both problems with a will. The reorganization of 1783–84 was more formal than previous combinations, and although it was neither a chartered corporation nor a limited liability company it was said to have been officially registered at Quebec. The great merchants, Benjamin and Joseph Frobisher and Simon McTavish, were entrusted with the general management of affairs, and the Frobishers styled themselves 'Directors'. Under their lead the Company set out to establish its position in the geopolitical situation which the peace had created.

During the peace negotiations and the subsequent discussions over the retention of the western posts, memorandum after memorandum came from this Northwest Company. Their strongest argument was that the members of the Company knew the lakes and the woods as no one else did, and that they would project English (as distinct from American) culture through the western lands. The Company would act as a defence against encroachment by the United States and would keep the middle west as a fur-trade reserve and as a market for the disposal of British goods. The last point, in particular, was sure of approval from the British statesmen of that time. But the Northwest Company did more than protest and lobby; in its efforts to circumvent the 'shameful terms' of the peace it took into its service a disgruntled Hudson's Bay man, Edward Umfreville, and sent him out in 1784 to find an alternative route to the Grand Portage. At the same time both the Frobishers and Peter Pond were underlining the dangers to be faced if the United States took effective possession of the ceded middle-west lands and gained predominance in the fur trade. Pond wrote with particular force, though with little skill (for he was almost illiterate). During his winter in Athabaska, working from Indian maps drawn on bark or in the sand, and from his own knowledge of the country, he had thought much about a river reported to run north (if anything northwest rather than northeast), which he concluded must come out to the Pacific. He had formulated a concept of a water route which would lead the British from Montreal to Lake Superior, then by Grand Portage to Lake Winnipeg and the Saskatchewan, over Portage la Loche to the Clearwater and so to Athabaska, and down his northern river to the Pacific. The northern river ultimately proved to be the Mackenzie, falling into the Arctic, not into the Pacific; but at the time (in 1785) the concept of a route to the Pacific became the main thesis in Pond's badly written but forceful petition for a monopoly of the northwest trade for the Northwest Company. In return for such a monopoly the Company would undertake the duty of discovering the route to the Pacific.

But the Northwest Company as it was set up in 1783–84 did not appeal to Peter Pond. It was strongly under the influence of the Montreal merchants, and as time passed it became even more so. Once more the trade was divided into sixteen shares, of which four were allotted to the Frobishers and two to their satellite Nicholas Montour (so that the Frobishers controlled six shares); Simon McTavish was allotted three shares and his subsidiary, Samuel Small, two (so that he controlled five shares). The two great firms therefore had eleven of the sixteen shares under their joint control and could put through any decision on which they were agreed. Pond, coming out from a winter in Athabaska, was offered a single share, which he refused. The offer remained open to him, and after another winter in Athabaska he took up his share in 1785.

The common stock of the new company was to run for five years, and the petitions and statements which are such a marked feature of this period make it possible to get some notion of the way in which the trade was managed under this system. The Northwest Company now claimed that its annual outlay in the purchase of goods amounted to about £25,000 of goods for the Indian country. The total capital in trade goods (exclusive of boats, posts, and equipment) would therefore be about £50,000; and with this outlay the company claimed to bring out about £100,000 of furs every year. The time schedule which the trade demanded was as interesting as the financial picture; and in 1784, when the Frobishers put in a petition for a monopoly for the Company, they explained that the Montreal merchants must start their consignments off from Montreal for the Grand Portage early in May. For this stage of the trade *canôts du maître* were used—big canoes with crews of eight to ten men and carrying perhaps as much as four tons. They would pause at Mackinac to replenish their food supplies and would then press on to the Grand Portage, where they must arrive early in July. Boats on the Great Lakes were also used for this stage of the trade, and they were the subject of some of the petitions which the Northwesters submitted, although they were not mentioned in the particular memorandum which the Frobishers submitted. At Grand Portage the winterers would have come down from their posts in their *canôts du nord*—smaller canoes with crews of only two or three men and carrying perhaps a ton-and-a-quarter of goods. Stopping at Grand Portage only long enough to stock up their canoes with the goods which the canôts du maître had brought so far, the winterers must then beat off over the Portage and up the rivers to their wintering-grounds. By employing something like five hundred men, and by constant attention to the time factor and to the need to keep its supply depot as far forward as possible, the Northwest Company managed to get its winterers out to their posts ahead of their rivals and before the northern rivers froze.

But the necessary routine left no latitude for inefficiency, and it emphasized the high cost of competition in the trade and (for the Northwesters) the need for uncompromising rivalry where competition created additional hazards. The arrangements of 1783–84 made such competition almost inevitable, for the partnership then formed excluded not only some of the small traders and winterers but some of the great merchant houses, who would be capable of financing an opposition and outfitting the excluded winterers. Chief among such winterers were Peter Pangman and John Ross (and Peter Pond for the first year), while the considerable merchant firm of Gregory, McLeod and Company was also left out of the partnership. They did business at Detroit as well as in Montreal, but they now turned to the northwest, where they had several posts. Their competition was a serious matter for the Northwest Company, for although they had fewer resources, they could command able traders, and they sent Pangman to the strategically sited Fort des Prairies, Alexander Mackenzie to Ile-à-la-Crosse, his cousin Roderick to Lac des Serpents, and John Ross to Athabaska. Ross was still in Athabaska for the winter 1786–87, when Peter Pond, now reconciled to the Northwest Company and using his share of the trade, came up to winter alongside him. After the death of Etienne Wadden and in view of his known character and the rumours which hung round his early career, anyone wintering alongside Peter Pond should have been particularly careful; but in the spring of 1787 Ross got into some sort of quarrel with Pond— and never lived to tell the tale. What happened is again not clear; but again the charge of murder was never brought home to Peter Pond.

The killing of John Ross was an unplanned act of violence by one individual and should not colour the whole picture of the opposition between Gregory, McLeod and Company and the Northwest Company. But it showed the lengths to which competition could take men, and the trade figures show the same determination to drive rivals out of the field at all costs. The figures for the rum and spirits sent to the upper country are particularly revealing. In 1785, Gregory, McLeod and Company were licenced to send up four canoes carrying four hundred gallons of rum and thirty-two gallons of wine, worth in all £2,850. Ross and Pangman, on a separate licence, also took up four canoes with thirty-two gallons of wine; but they took only three hundred and fifty gallons of rum, and their total cost was only £2,775. Against this combined supply of seven hundred and fifty gallons of rum and combined expenditure of £5,625, the Northwest Company was licenced to take up twenty-five canoes and four batteaux with six thousand gallons of rum, three hundred and forty gallons of wine, and other goods to a value of £20,500. Such figures support the Company's statement that in general their trade ran at a level of about £25,000 goods purchased in an average year, and they show the Company's predominance over even substantial and organized rivals.

In the field, competition was met by giving Indians more liquor and more trade goods for their furs; but this spoiled the trade. Competition was also met by uncompromising hostility, which varied with the personalities engaged but which could reach the point at which murder was committed; and this roused comment and criticism and split the copartnership. Debauching Indians and terrorizing opponents were, indeed, costly and dangerous expedients which damaged the reputation of the Company and hindered it in its most ambitious attempts to end competition by seeking a grant of monopoly from government.

In these memoranda and petitions Peter Pond and his ideas occupied a key position. He was the man who had formulated the notion of the river route to the Pacific, which the Company was to discover and develop in return for a monopoly. But Peter Pond had become a liability rather than an asset, and when the news of Ross's death precipitated a re-formation of the Northwest Company in 1787 he was (again) not a member. He was important enough to be offered a share, but he sold it to McTavish's nephew, William McGillivray. Alexander Mackenzie was also allotted a share, for the reorganization was in itself a move to end competition by the absorption into the Northwest Company of the rival firm. Both sides, it was said, had already incurred serious losses, and in 1787 they were united lest they should destroy each other.

With the inclusion of Gregory, McLeod and Company, the Northwesters now increased the number of their shares to twenty. But still preponderance lay with the great Montreal houses; Simon McTavish held four shares and Joseph Frobisher (now alone in the family concern) three, while their supporters Patrick Small and Nicholas Montour held two each—a total of eleven out of twenty, with McTavish as the largest individual shareholder. Their preponderance was enhanced when, in November of 1787, Simon McTavish and Joseph Frobisher combined their merchandising businesses to form the firm of McTavish, Frobisher and Company. This concern proved capable of dominating the Northwest Company and, indeed, the whole of the Montreal fur trade. The two partners held controlling shares in the Northwest Company, and they allocated to their own firm the lucrative business of acting as the Company's agents, charged with shipping out to Canada all the goods required by the Company. At the same time McTavish formed and controlled the London firm of McTavish, Fraser and Company, supplying most of the capital and taking two-thirds of the profits. In this way he put the London end of the Northwest Company's business into the hands of his own company—and of his grossly overworked junior partner and relative, John Fraser. The London office not only had to order supplies for the Northwesters and dispose of their furs but also had its own private business.

At each reorganization the Northwest Company had gained in control and in unity of purpose; and at each reorganization it had been spurred on by a geographical problem. Despite the great weight of the merchant interests in the reorganization of 1787 these things remained true. Though Peter Pond sold his share (and took himself off to the United States, where he discussed his ideas with the savants of Yale and even tried to interest Congress in his route to the Pacific), his purpose was deliberately taken up by the Company and engrossed it for the rest of its career. The young winterer from Gregory, McLeod and Company, Alexander Mackenzie, took over the prosecution of Pond's ideas, and the Company fully supported him. A route to the Pacific would have great prestige value and would improve the Company's chances of securing a monopoly (or so it was thought), and it held promise of enormous profit also. The great wealth of sea-otter skins on the northern Pacific coast of America had been revealed when the survivors from Vitus Bering's last fatal voyage had taken some of the skins back from the Aleutians to Kamchatka in 1742, and the possibilities of selling these furs on the markets of China were developed in several subsequent voyages by both British and American ships. The importance of a trade in furs across the Pacific to China increased steadily through the years, while the voyages of Cook and Vancouver (and the Nootka Sound incident in 1790) focused attention on the Pacific coast. For the Northwesters China became an additional attraction as the European market was upset, first by the outbreak of war between Turkey and Russia in 1787, then by the wars of the French Revolution, and finally by Napoleon's dominance in Europe. The London market became overstocked, furs were difficult to sell—and the route to the Pacific, and so to China, demanded attention.

For this purpose Athabaska was both the springboard from which any exploration must start and the source of the trade which must pay for such speculation. Peter Pond had been the pioneer there. For the moment he was finding little welcome for his notions in the United States, for the Louisiana Purchase had not yet given the opportunity for access to the Rockies, and 'Manifest Destiny' was not yet an accepted doctrine. In his place Alexander Mackenzie was sent into Athabaska by the new concern; and once more the first step towards further expansion was to advance the supply depot. Fort Chipewyan was set up as the 'emporium of the north' in 1788, and in 1789 Mackenzie started from that post to seek the Pacific, as Pond had planned. Actually the river running north from Great Slave Lake, the Mackenzie, led the explorer not to the Pacific but to the Arctic, and in 1790 he returned to the Grand Portage disappointed and to some extent discountenanced. He faced the conclusion that since there was no river in the north which would lead him around the northern extremity of the Rockies he must work more westward and find a way through the mountains. He was determined to continue his explorations, and to equip himself for the task. In the meantime he lost a great deal of the friend-

ship and confidence of the partners of the Northwest
Company, for the Company was geared to the policy of
finding the route to the Pacific, and in that context
Mackenzie's journey to the Arctic was a failure.

This setback for the Company played its part in pre-
cipitating changes in the organization, for it accentuated
the differences in outlook and in experience between the
winterers and the agents. Mackenzie himself spent the
winter of 1791–92 in England, mastering the techniques
of surveying; and he was promised an extra share in the
Company in a plan for reform and expansion which was
drawn up in 1790 (but which never came into effect).
But he was not the only winterer who felt disgruntled,
and when the five-year contract of 1787 ran out in 1792
the reorganization within the Company had to be much
more drastic than the agents had originally anticipated.
For this the explanation must be sought both in the
circumstances of the all-important trade to Athabaska
(which emphasized the qualities and the claims of the
winterers), and also in the circumstances of the American frontier. There the discussions which culminated in
Jay's Treaty were coming to a head, and the southwest
fur traders were being faced with their final decision—
whether to throw in their lot definitively with the southwest trade under American control or to turn to the
northwest and remain under Canadian and British control. It was becoming clear that American control would
result in 'A Systematic Plan to drive the British Indian
Traders from the American Territory by every species
of vexation', and against this the prosperity which was
being achieved by the Northwest Company was a

strong attraction. One of the southwest men, John McGill, reckoned that members of the Northwest Company were making £3,000 profit a year on each share which they held in the trade, and a group of powerful southwesters made 'direct and serious applications for a Concern in the N.W.'.

The southwesters' applications could not be ignored; for they were men of substance, and they were already financing competition in the northwest. In a petition of 1791 the three firms of McTavish, Frobisher and Company, Forsyth, Richardson and Company, and Todd, McGill and Company told Lieutenant-Governor Simcoe that they were the principal firms of Montreal and that between them they controlled two-thirds of the trade of the city. Of the three giants, Forsyth, Richardson and Company, and Todd, McGill and Company were primarily concerned with the southwest trade but were alarmed at the prospects there and anxious, at that time, to claim a share in the trade to the northwest. To some extent their views were met, and the Northwest Company as set up in 1792 (to last for seven years) included such southwesters as Forsyth, Richardson and Company, Todd, McGill and Company, and the Henry firm of Alexander Henry and his nephew (the younger Alexander). The new concern divided its business into forty-six shares to make room for the new arrivals; and in the arrangement Alexander Mackenzie was allotted six shares, for it was an expanding trade, still geared to the Pacific approach, which the reorganized company sought.

For a time this comprehensive arrangement worked,

G

and worked well. Under its auspices, and using its resources, Alexander Mackenzie made his way from Athabaska up the Peace River into the heart of the Rockies,
over the summit, and by the tumultuous Fraser River to
within striking distance of the Pacific. He finished the
last stage on foot, and at Bella Coola Sound he left his
mark—'Alexander Mackenzie, from Canada, by land,
the twenty-second of July, one thousand seven hundred
and ninety-three.' Again Mackenzie's great exploration
proved little to the point where the Northwest Company
was concerned. His route was dangerous and useless for
the fur trade and once more he was left feeling frustrated
and slighted. The predominance of the agents within
the Company, especially McTavish and his relations,
seemed to entail too little attention to the needs and the
claims of the winterers and the explorers, such as
Mackenzie.

Mackenzie, however he might feel, was tied to the
Northwest Company until the 1792 agreement should
expire in 1799. In the meantime, McTavish was greatly
taken up with his affairs in London and was becoming
remote and increasingly arbitrary. The Company,
which had counted so much on the opening of a trade to
China, not only saw Mackenzie's journey as a costly
failure but was also faced with heavy losses on shipments
from Boston to that market. The Northwest Company's
'Adventure to China' carried an adverse balance of
£23,000 by 1794 and the reality of American opposition
in the China trade was clear from the co-operation with
Americans (especially with John Jacob Astor) which
had been forced on the Northwesters in order to or-

ganize their shipments through Boston. The complexities involved as the Company's business spread round the world were beyond the understanding of all except the professional administrators, and beyond the confidence of all save McTavish's devoted followers. Disgruntlement was again spreading among the winterers; and although division within the Company inevitably took on a strong personal colour, it was derived basically from the difficulties of the route from Montreal to the Pacific and thence to China.

It is not surprising, in view of these problems, that the agreement of 1792 should have been substantially modified in 1795. In that year Todd, McGill and Company gave up their aspirations in the northwest, accepted the consequences of Jay's Treaty, and were not included in the new arrangement. The other important southwest firm which had been accepted into the Northwest Company in 1792 (Forsyth, Richardson and Company) was also disillusioned with its experience and stood outside the new arrangement. But this firm retained its interest in the northwest trade and stood ready to finance, and to act as agent for, opposition traders. So the American frontier and Jay's Treaty had brought to the northwest trade a great agency house; and although considerable 'sacrifices' were made to placate the winterers and allot shares to them in the copartnership which McTavish reorganized in 1795, many of them remained disgruntled. They had available the financial backing of Forsyth, Richardson and Company (and of other firms), and they had the leadership of Alexander Mackenzie.

Though the most obvious results of this crisis were to

be seen as opposition was mobilized on the routes to Athabaska, at the posts from which furs and profits were derived, and through the Rocky Mountains to the Pacific, the problems of the trade were also accentuated nearer to Montreal. There competition to secure canoes, canoemen, and food for the long and exhausting journeys occupied much attention, and although the Northwest Company's affairs lay so largely in the control of the merchants, they showed a realistic appreciation of the physical difficulties of the trade. Under the new régime much care was devoted to improvements in transportation. This was the period when the Northwest Company was launching ships on the Great Lakes, planning and building a canal at Sault Ste. Marie, building roads over the portages on the Ottawa River, and employing another Hudson's Bay man, David Thompson, to survey the American frontier accurately and to search for an alternative route to the Grand Portage. Substantial and effective effort went into all these aspects of the trade, and for the Northwest Company the period between 1794 and 1798 was undoubtedly a period of organized progress—organized not only against rival traders but also against the physical obstacles in the trade.

But there were 'Free Traders' in the northwest, and powerful merchant houses arrayed behind the traders. The opposition took more definite shape in 1798 when Forsyth, Richardson and Company, with Leith, Jamieson and Company, made a formal agreement with a group of six winterers and so set on foot the so-called New Northwest Company. In the course of its brief career this organization was also dubbed the XY Company (from the mark put on its bales of goods, to distinguish them in transit from those marked 'NW Company'); and when the great explorer was freed from his agreement with the Old Northwest Company in 1799, and joined and led the new concern it was often called 'Alexander Mackenzie and Company'. Rivalry between the old and the new Northwest Companies speedily reached an intensity which had never been equalled. The crime and the debauching of Indians which resulted were such as to lead to the Canada Jurisdiction Act of 1803, which placed the Indian territories under the jurisdiction of the courts of Canada. It was an inspiring period, but it had its unattractive aspects, and the hostility which animated it lasted through a regrouping of the Old Northwest Company in 1799 and a further regrouping in 1802, until the losses suffered by both concerns, and the death of Simon McTavish in 1804, made an amalgamation both possible and necessary in 1805.

During the period of hostility the outrageous conduct of the Indian trade absorbs attention and obscures the fact that the two Montreal concerns were absorbed in rivalry for something of greater significance than their race to secure the hunts of the Athabaskan (and other) Indians. Mackenzie's route to the Pacific was indeed of no serious value to the fur trade. It must be improved on. But any new route would still start from Athabaska, or perhaps from the upper reaches of the Saskatchewan, and would lead into the Rockies in a southwesterly direction. If, as was inescapable, both Northwest Companies accepted that the all-important brigades for the Pacific must start out from Athabaska, then they were forced also to accept the fact that the long haul from Montreal to Athabaska was a handicap. That route must be abandoned, and the approach to Athabaska from Hudson's Bay must be accepted as the only sensible alternative. Logically this should have led also to the conclusion that control would need to be transferred to London, for shipment from London to Montreal and then to the Bay made little sense as against the advantages of direct shipment from London, and management should lie at one terminus of the transport route or the other, not at some external point such as Montreal would become. For the moment this conclusion did not seem to be realized; but as they accepted the fact that the best route to Athabaska lay through Hudson's Bay and its rivers, both Northwest Companies accentuated their rivalry to the Hudson's Bay Company and became involved in attempts to encroach on its chartered rights.

Alexander Mackenzie exploited his reputation to gain the ear of British statesmen for his project of a comprehensive fur and fishing company, which should enjoy the Hudson's Bay Company's amenities, while the leaders of the old Northwest Company worked in the same direction by sending their own ship to the Bay in order to challenge the legality of the Hudson's Bay Company's charter. Duncan McGillivray and Edward Ellice took up this move in London, and since the Hudson's Bay Company was hard hit by the Napoleonic Wars and the loss of the European market, and was under apathetic management, it appeared to be quite possible that the Northwesters might either force a concession or even be able to buy controlling shares in the chartered company. Mackenzie and Ellice turned to the latter course, and in their early operations they found a collaborator in the Earl of Selkirk. Only when Selkirk revealed that his true intention was not to hand over the Hudson's Bay Company to Northwest management but to use its vast charter as the basis for colonization at the Red River, a crucial spot in the Northwest Company's existing transport system, did the Northwesters turn against him. By then the Northwest Company was dominated by William McGillivray, nephew and heir-in-office of Simon McTavish, a man who had enjoyed wintering experience in Athabaska and elsewhere before being recalled to Montreal for management. He brought to the struggle a 'Northwest Spirit' which fully exploited both the adventurousness and the efficiency of his Company and which, by its capacity for intimidation, its contemptuous assertiveness, and its legalistic opportunism, produced the Massacre of Seven Oaks and the dispersal of Selkirk's colonists. The answer was the capture of Fort William by Selkirk, and of a group of Northwest partners by Governor Williams of the Hudson's Bay Company; and the disruption of the Northwest trade, which was already unbalanced by the costs of competition. The climax came with a series of inconclusive and unsatisfactory trials held in Montreal, with a Governor-General's Commission to inquire into affairs in the Indian territory and with a Parliamentary Blue Book.

It was inevitable at that time, and it has been inevitable since, that attention should be focused on the personalities involved and on the fierceness of the struggle—above all that we should be fascinated by the bitterness of the Northwesters' opposition to the Red River Colony and by the clash of character between William McGillivray and the Earl of Selkirk. The ultimate outcome was the so-called 'Coalition' between the Northwest and the Hudson's Bay Companies (arranged in 1820); and such an outcome to a struggle between the magnificent, comprehensive, and virile organization which had developed at Montreal and the disheartened and indifferent coterie (none of them fur traders in the Northwest meaning of the term) which enjoyed the Hudson's Bay charter, may seem odd. Technical ability, imagination, and volume of trade all lay on the side of the Northwesters. The explanation depends in part on the internal circumstances of the Northwest Company; for the agents had alienated and worried a substantial body of the winterers by their conduct of the struggle. They had also over-reached themselves financially; and the partnership negotiated in 1805 was coming to its end. Notwithstanding appearances, the Northwest Company was exceedingly vulnerable, and the achievement of anything which would bear the appearance of a 'coalition' was in itself something of a triumph. But the Hudson's Bay Company had in a fortunate hour fallen into the hands of determined and competent executives; and the reason why the Northwest Company did not submerge its opponent was exactly the same, basically geographical reason which made the struggle necessary in the first place.

The Hudson's Bay Company could claim exclusive control of the Bayside route to Athabaska (and so to the Pacific). If, as proved to be the case, it could muster sufficient strength and purpose to maintain that right, then the Northwest challenge was doomed to failure. In the long run, whoever controlled that route would dominate Canada's fur trade; and an analysis of the shares in which the trade was apportioned after the 'coalition' makes it clear that in effect the 'coalition' placed the Northwesters' trade under the control of the Hudson's Bay Company. The subsequent organization and management of the fur-trade empire so created makes this conclusion even more clear. The outcome in geographical terms was inescapable. When (for the first time in its long history) the Hudson's Bay Company sent a Director to Rupert's Land to arrange the details of the joint trade, he completely vindicated the superior claims of the Bayside route over Montreal. This again was an outcome which ran contrary to appearances. Nicholas Garry, the Hudson's Bay man, was religious, honest, sweet, and rather simple. He was shrewd after the manner of London's city gentry, but no one would have thought him a match for William and Simon McGillivray. He seems to have been chosen largely because he was the only bachelor on the board; and he finished his life in an unbalanced state of mind. But his diary of his journey reveals the way in which the determined and experienced Northwest agents set out to preserve the claims of the agency business run from Montreal, and the way in which they failed.

From 1820 onward Montreal remained important in

the fur trade—but no longer dominant for geographical reasons. It still provided a starting-point from which managerial personnel, orders, and reports could be sent by a comparatively rapid but expensive route into the northwest. That is the reason why George Simpson made Lachine his residence and headquarters in the next generation, and why, during the unprecedented exploitation of the fur trade of Canada which he organized, Montreal was the point of departure for the express canoes which ranged the north. But as a transport route the Montreal approach to Athabaska was superseded and subordinated. The goods for trade with the Indians were shipped into North America by way of Hudson's Bay. With an open choice between the two routes, the management of the 'coalition' forsook Montreal except for occasions when considerations of speed overrode those of cost. For reasons which even the great knowledge and determination of the Northwesters could not overcome, Montreal had ceased to be the supply centre of the fur trade.

Suggestions for further reading:

CAMPBELL, M. W. *The North West Company*. Toronto: Toronto University Press, 1957.

CHITTENDEN, H. M. *The American Fur Trade of the Far West*. 3 vols. New York: F. P. Harper, 1902.

DAVIDSON, G. C. *The North West Company*. Berkeley, California: California University Press, 1918.

FLEMING, R. HARVEY. 'McTavish, Frobisher and Company of Montreal', *Canadian Historical Review*, X (June 1929), 136–52.

—— 'The Origin of "Sir Alexander Mackenzie and Company" ', *Canadian Historical Review*, IX (June 1928), 137–55.

GRAY, J. M. *Lord Selkirk of Red River*. Toronto: Macmillan, 1963.

INNIS, H. A. *Peter Pond; Fur Trader and Adventurer*. Toronto: Irwin & Gordon, 1930.

LAWSON, M. G. *Fur, A Study in English Mercantilism, 1700–1775*. Toronto: Toronto University Press, 1943.

MACKENZIE, ALEXANDER. *Voyages from Montreal on the River St. Lawrence through the Continent of North America*. 2 vols. Toronto: Radisson Society, 1927.

MORTON, A. S. *A History of the Canadian West to 1870–71*. London: Nelson, 1939.

RICH, E. E. *The History of the Hudson's Bay Company, 1670–1870*. 2 vols. London: Hudson's Bay Record Society, 1958–59.

WALLACE, W. S. ed. *Documents Relating to the North West Company*. Toronto: Champlain Society, 1934.